The Jodie Davis
Needle Arts School

Teach

Yourself

Teddy Bear

Making

The Jodie Davis Needle Arts School

Teach

SIMPLE TECHNIQUES

Yourself

AND PATTERNS

Teddy Bear

FOR TEDDY BEARS

Making

AND THEIR CLOTHING

JODIE DAVIS

PHOTOGRAPHS BY BILL MILNE

FRIEDMAN/FAIRFAX
PUBLISHERS

A FRIEDMAN/FAIRFAX BOOK

© 1996 by Michael Friedman Publishing Group, Inc.

Library of Congress Cataloging-in-Publication data available upon request.

ISBN 1-56799-256-0

Project Editor: Elizabeth Viscott Sullivan
Editor: Jackie Smyth
Art Director: Lynne Yeamans
Design: Elan Studio
Photography Director: Christopher C. Bain
Illustrator: Barbara Henning
Production Coordinator Marnie Ann Boardman

Every effort has been made to present the information in this book in a clear, complete, and accurate manner. It is important that all instructions be carefully followed as failure to do so could result in injury and the publisher and the author expressly disclaim any and all liability resulting therefrom. The author also suggests refraining from using glass, bead, or button eyes on bears intended for small children.

Color separations by Excel Graphic Arts Ltd.
Printed in China by Leefung-Asco Printers Ltd.

For bulk purchases and special sales, please contact:
Friedman/Fairfax Publishers
Attention: Sales Department
15 West 26th Street
New York, NY 10010
(212) 685-6610 • FAX (212) 685-1307

To Mom and Don

Acknowledgments

Thanks to Ron Block of Edinburgh Imports for kindly supplying me with many of the furs and bear-making supplies used to make the bears in this book.

Thanks to Christie and Steve for putting up with us (the bears and me).

contents

Introduction

Teach Yourself Teddy Bear Making is a craft class in a book. Begin with the first bear, and by the end of the book you'll be an experienced teddy bear maker!

the magic of teddy bears

As with all classes, there are prerequisites for learning to make teddy bears. In this case, that means basic sewing skills and the desire to create teddy bears. With these in hand, the budding teddy bear maker is in for a lot of fun!

Sewing a teddy bear does differ from sewing a garment. Yes, stitching fur is different from stitching fabric. And stuffing, jointing, and other specialized techniques are involved. But what I'm getting at is the magic you feel as the bear takes shape in your hands; that involuntary "Aha!" feeling when those pieces of fabric you are sewing together take on a personality.

One of the wonders of bear making is that no matter how carefully you trace the patterns, no matter how you try to replicate the materials I have used, your teddy bear will reflect *your* personality. That is what I wish to share with you.

how to use this book

I designed this book in a learn-as-you-go fashion. The first chapter, The Bear Basics, covers the information you will need to know before you begin your first bear. Lists of equipment and supplies and general information about preparing patterns and furs will send you on your way.

Jump right into bear making with a one-pattern-piece bear in chapter two. In creating this first bear, you will learn to mark, stitch, turn, and stuff.

Subsequent chapters offer more bear patterns, along with variations, each requiring additional skills. All projects are clearly illustrated with full instructions. My hope is that by the end of the book you will feel confident enough to try your hand at creating your own original bears.

So join me in this bear-making class. And when you've completed a bear or two, please share it with me.

Jodie Davis
Boca Raton, Florida

chapter one

The Bear Basics

This chapter includes all the information you will need to get

started making your first bear. ❀   Most of the equipment

and supplies   listed here are needed for making all

the bears in the book. Many of the necessary   tools can be found

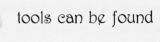

around the house. Some bears will require   additional mate-

rials and supplies—check the instructions for the specific bear

you are making to determine exactly what you will need.

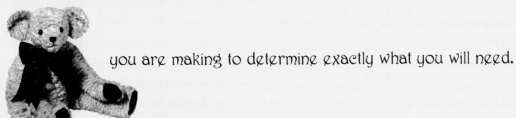

equipment

* **Sewing machine**
* **Machine needles size 14 (90) or 16 (100)**
* **Dressmaker's shears**
* **Paper scissors**
* **Straight pins**
* **Hand sewing needles**
* **Long dollmaker's needle (see Sources, page 124)**
* **Bear brush (see Sources, page 124)**
* **Stuffing tools (see Sources, page 124)**
* **Marking pens (see Sources, page 124)**

supplies

* **Sewing thread**
* **Waxed dental floss or carpet thread**
* **Polyester fiberfill stuffing**
* **Fray Check™ seam sealant**
* **Template material: cereal boxes, Mylar, or used file folders**
* **Unlined paper**

preparing patterns

To use the bear and clothing patterns in this book, trace the patterns onto paper, or photocopy them. If you photocopy them, be sure to first determine whether the machine copies accurately by making a copy and comparing it to the original.

Some of the patterns were too large to fit on one page, so I cut these apart and placed them on adjacent pages. The number of parts needed to complete the pattern and the edges at which they should be joined are marked on the pieces.

Cut out the pattern copies roughly, leaving extra paper outside the lines. Glue the patterns to cereal boxes, Mylar, file folders, or any material strong enough to withstand repeated use. With paper scissors, cut through both thicknesses along the outside edges of the pattern lines.

fur selection

Fur fabrics are made of either synthetic or natural fibers on a knit or woven backing, and are usually 58 or 60 inches (147.5 or 152.5cm) wide.

A knit backing has lengthwise stretch, woven backing crosswise, or bias, stretch. Because of this, the same bear pattern made twice, once in each of these fabrics, will look different.

A limited choice of synthetic furs is available in most local fabric shops. Although I am pleasantly surprised once in a while, for the most part these furs are of inferior quality. Many times, the backing doesn't spring back when stretched. And when I fold the fabric I can see the backing—indicating that the pile isn't at all dense, a sure sign of inferior quality and an anemic bear waiting to happen.

High-quality, luxurious synthetic furs are more readily available from the specialty bear wares suppliers listed in the Sources section (see page 124). These furs are dense, of dreamy quality, and have a woven backing for added stability; they are well worth the added investment.

Natural fiber furs, such as mohair, alpaca, or cotton, as well as rayon offer a spectrum of bear-making possibilities. Bear suppliers search far and wide to locate new, inspiring furs, and are the most reliable source for high-quality materials.

An important consideration is pile height. A variation in pile height will change the appearance of the finished bear, which may or may not be an advantage.

Fur fabrics are available in a wide range of colors, as well as color variations. "Tipped" fur has a second color on the end of every strand.

Distressed, swirled, sparse mohair for a well-loved look, cotton "string" fabric—there are many exciting options for the bear maker. Send for some samples—you'll be inspired!

Since it is much easier to sew to short pile fur, use short pile fur for your first bear.

Roni Gerhardt, Delevan, New Jersey

working with fur

To find the nap of the fur, stroke it as you would a dog. Lay the fabric, with the backing side up, flat on a table. Line all the pattern pieces on the fabric with the arrows on the patterns pointing in the direction of the nap of the fur, toward the dog's

tail. The arrows should then be aligned with the grain of the backing. Use quilting pins or pattern weights to hold the pattern pieces in place.

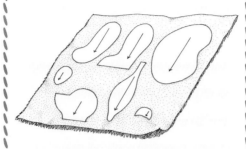

cutting fur

Cut a single layer of fur at a time. Make small snips with your shears, cutting only the backing, not the fur pile. Cut just inside the traced lines.

To cut down on annoying stray fur, put the teddy bear pieces in the dryer on low heat for a few minutes after cutting them out. You can then scoop the stray fur from the edges of the fur from the lint filter rather than your sewing room floor.

Kathy Semone, Rockville, Maryland

stitching fur

Choose a size 14(90) or 16(100) needle for your sewing machine. Thread the machine with regular sewing thread of high quality. Shorten the stitch length slightly, to about 12 stitches per inch (2.5cm).

If you haven't sewn fur before, you will find it seems bulky and awkward at first, so practice on scraps before beginning your bear. Most sewing machines will have no trouble with it, and soon you'll be comfortable with the feel of sewing the fur.

finishing pile

After assembling your bear, use a long dollmaking needle to release the pile trapped in the seams.

A nifty tool for this job is the bear brush available from the suppliers listed in the Sources section (page 124). A small version of a dog brush, this item does a wonderful job of freeing any pile caught in seams. Don't be afraid to scrub back and forth along the seams with the brush. Also, use the brush to further conceal the seams after ladderstitching them closed.

the lost thread method

Often in bear making it is necessary to end a thread as inconspicuously as possible.

I like to finish off my ladderstitching when closing body openings and my embroidery with what I call the lost thread method.

To do this, I push my needle into the fabric at the end of my last stitch and come up an inch (2.5cm) or so away. Then I push my needle back into the fabric just a few threads over from where it just came out. This stitch will be unseen, especially considering the masking quality of the fur pile. I repeat this, then emerge from the fabric again and clip the thread close to the backing. This effectively loses the thread end inside the bear and secures it at the same time.

chapter two

One-Pattern-Piece Bear

Finished size: 13¹/₂ inches (34.2cm)

This super-simple pattern works up in a jiffy.

The easy construction and few pattern

pieces belie the charm this little bear holds. ✿ Fabric options

abound for this bear. In addition to the tried-and-true fur fabrics,

branch out and try terry cloth, Polarfleece®,

or even a heavy knit.

materials

* **16 × 18-inch (40.6 × 45.7cm) piece of fabric**
* **Matching thread**
* **Contrasting fabric for muzzle, if desired**
* **Two ¹/₂-inch (1.2cm) safety eyes or buttons**
* **Polyester fiberfill**
* **Embroidery floss or perle cotton**

instructions

1 Prepare the patterns as instructed on pages 12 and 13.

2 Fold the fabric in half so that the right sides face one another, matching the shorter edges. Lay the paper pattern on the fabric, aligning the arrow with the direction of the nap. Trace around the pattern. Remove the pattern. Pin the two layers together inside the traced lines.

Marking Tools

A permanent black pen, such as a Sharpie or Pigma, is a safe choice for tracing around patterns and transferring markings onto fur backing. For white fabrics I use a disappearing marker. The purple markings do vanish within a day, so I make up my bear quickly. For black or very dark brown fabrics, use a white dressmaker's pencil or a silver quilting pencil.

3 Stitch all the way around just inside the marked lines, leaving an opening between the dots on one inner leg for turning and stuffing.

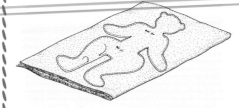

4 Trim the seam allowances to about ³/₈ inch (1cm). Clip into the seam allowance at the underarms and between the legs as shown.

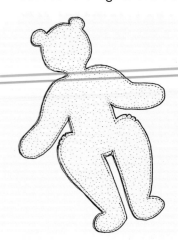

5 Turn the bear right side out.

6 If using safety eyes, install them now, following the instructions on page 46.

7 Stuff the bear, beginning with the ears. Stuff the ears softly. Cut the ears off the bear pattern along the top stitching markings. Place them on the bear and follow the cut edge as a guide for topstitching. Stuff the arm firmly. To make a template for the topstitching at the neck, arms, and legs, trim the arms, legs, and head from the bear pattern along the marked stitching lines. Pin the remaining portion, the bear's body, to the bear. Topstitch along the edge of the paper where you cut the stitching line for the arm. Repeat for the remaining arm, one leg, and the head.

Stuff the body. Topstitch across the top of the remaining leg.

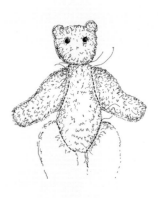

Stuff the remaining leg. Ladderstitch the opening in the leg closed.

Closing Openings

Ladderstitch

For a virtually invisible seam closure, use a ladderstitch.

Work from the right side of the fabric. Do not turn the seam allowances to the inside before stitching. They will turn naturally as the stitches are pulled tight.

Knot the end of a single strand of dental floss or quilting thread. From inside the bear, push the needle up through the fabric about 1/4 inch (6mm) below one end of the opening.

Go into the fabric close to where you came out. Come up about 1/8 inch (3mm) closer to the opening.

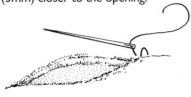

Take a stitch measuring about 1/8 inch (3mm) along the seamline on one side of the opening.

Cross over to the other side of the opening and take another 1/8-inch (3mm)-long stitch along the seam line, about 1/8 inch (3mm) farther along the opening.

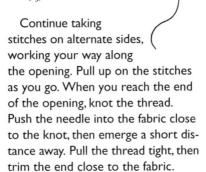

Continue taking stitches on alternate sides, working your way along the opening. Pull up on the stitches as you go. When you reach the end of the opening, knot the thread. Push the needle into the fabric close to the knot, then emerge a short distance away. Pull the thread tight, then trim the end close to the fabric.

Whipstitch

A whipstitch is used where an invisible seam isn't necessary and speed in stitching is a plus. This is the stitch I use to close the bottom of bear's ears. You can leave the thread attached after whipstitching and go right on to stitching the ears to the head.

Knot the end of a single strand of carpet or quilting thread or dental floss.

Turn the seam allowances to the inside.

Push the needle into the fabric along the fold at one end of the opening and through the fabric at the other side.

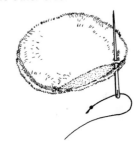

Repeat along the opening, making the stitches about 1/8 inch (3mm) apart.

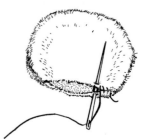

Knot the thread, but leave it attached, ready for sewing the ear to the head.

8 Machine baste around the round muzzle piece. Pull up on the threads to loosely gather. Using a small piece of stuffing, lightly stuff the muzzle. Pull up on the threads again. Tie the ends of the threads together. Pin the muzzle to the bear's face and hand sew in place.

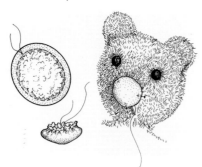

9 If using button eyes, hand sew them to the bear's face now.

10 To embroider the nose and mouth, cut the triangular nose pattern from paper. Place on the face. A dab from a glue stick will keep it in place. Thread a needle with embroidery floss and knot one end. Push the needle into the muzzle under the nose pattern. Come up at the left-hand top of the nose. Pull on the thread, concealing the knot under the nose pattern. Go back into the muzzle at the top right corner of the pattern and

emerge at the left, just below the first stitch. Continue in this manner, following the edge of the pattern.

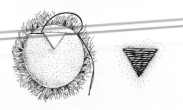

When you finish stitching the nose, emerge from the muzzle at the center bottom of the nose pattern. Stitch the mouth as shown. (Refer to page 75 for complete instructions.)

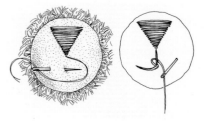

Remove the paper template, using tweezers to slide it from beneath the stitches.

After finishing the mouth, bring the needle out close to the muzzle but in the body. Knot the thread, then push the needle back into the fabric and come out again. Pull the thread so it will pop inside the bear, then trim the thread.

11 Optional: to make a contrasting tummy, baste around the tummy piece. Pull up on the threads to turn the seam allowance to the inside. Hand sew the tummy to the front of the bear.

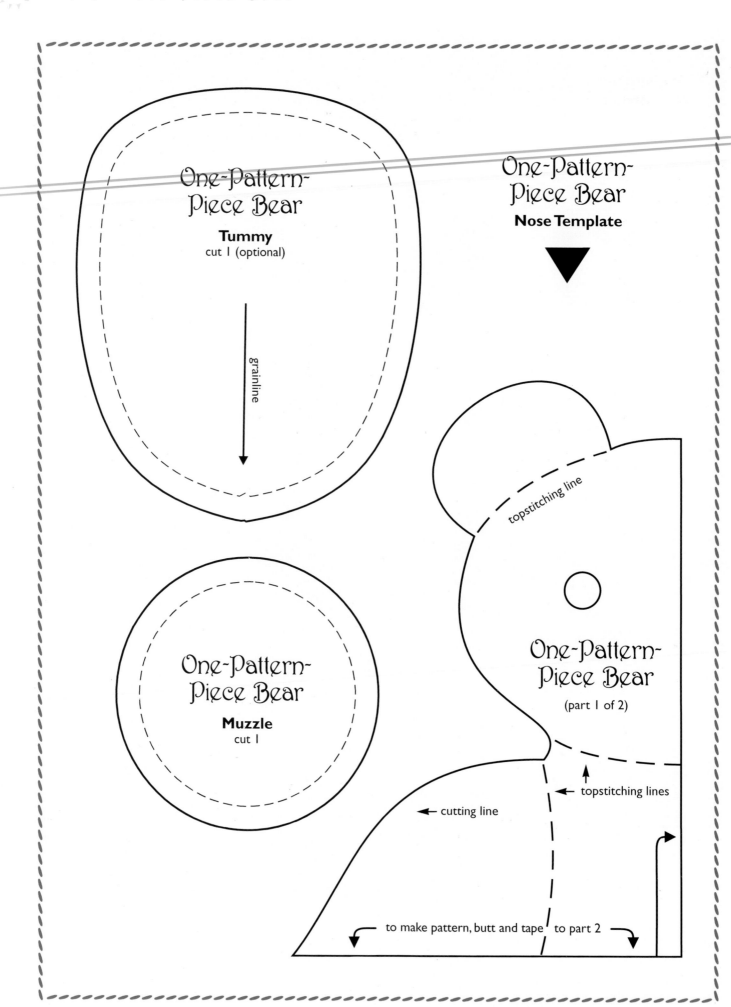

One-Pattern-
Piece Bear

Tummy
cut 1 (optional)

grainline

One-Pattern-
Piece Bear
Nose Template

One-Pattern-
Piece Bear

Muzzle
cut 1

topstitching line

One-Pattern-
Piece Bear

(part 1 of 2)

← cutting line

↑ topstitching lines

to make pattern, butt and tape   to part 2

**For cutting
see instructions**

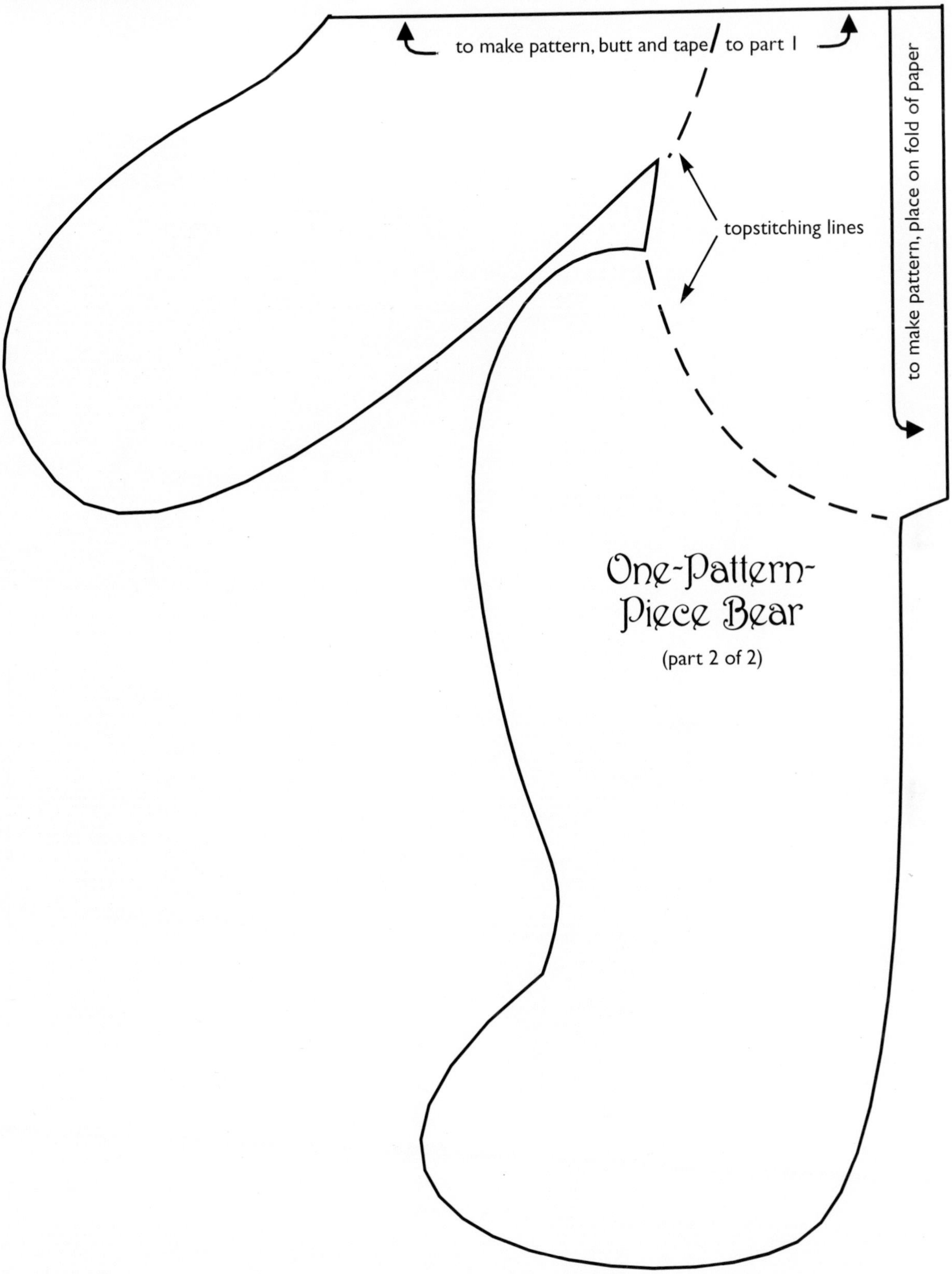

to make pattern, butt and tape to part I

topstitching lines

to make pattern, place on fold of paper

One-Pattern-
Piece Bear

(part 2 of 2)

chapter three

Snuggly Nonjointed Bear with Clothing

Finished size: 14 inches (35.5cm)

Dressed or not, this bear requires a bit more sewing experience

than the first bear. This slightly more skilled sewing affords a more

realistic bear. ❀ In making this bear, you will learn more about

stuffing bears, including  the option of filling

the bear with plastic pellets to  give the bear heft and make it poseable.

❀ Clothing patterns for both a boy and a girl bear make this a very versatile design.

materials

* ¹/₃ **yard (30.5cm) of fabric**
* **Matching thread**
* **8-inch (20.5cm) -square piece of contrasting fabric**
* **Polyester fiberfill stuffing**
* **Two 14mm safety eyes**
* **One 22mm plastic bear nose**
* **One ¹/₂-inch (1.2cm) -square piece of suede, felt, or leather to cover nose**
* **3 pounds (1.3kg) plastic stuffing pellets (optional)**

instructions

Note: All seam allowances are ¹/₄ inch (6mm) unless otherwise noted.

❶ Prepare the patterns and mark and cut out the fur as instructed on pages 12 and 13.

❷ Pin the paw pads to the inner arm pieces. Stitch.

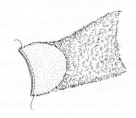

❸ Pin the inner arm pieces to the body front. Stitch.

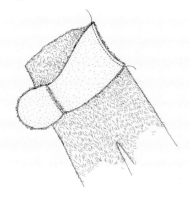

❹ Fold one body front along the leg dart fold line so that the right sides of the fur are together. Stitch along the curved dart stitching line.

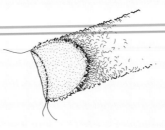

❺ Stitch the center back seam of the body back top from the dot down.

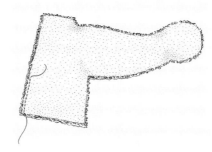

❻ Pin the body back bottom to the body back top, matching the dots at the corners. Stitch between the dots.

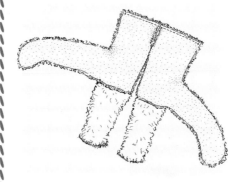

❼ Right sides together, pin the body back to the body front. Stitch, leaving the neck and the feet open.

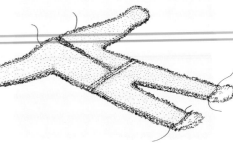

❽ Right sides together, pin a foot pad to the bottom of one leg, matching large dots to large dots and small dots to small dots. Ease to fit. Stitch.

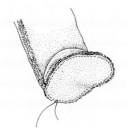

❾ Right sides together, stitch the two head back pieces together from the top to the dot.

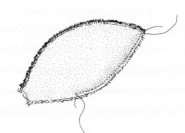

❿ Pin the muzzle to the head front, matching the dots. Ease to fit. Stitch.

11 Right sides together, fold the head front/muzzle, matching the raw edges. Stitch, leaving an opening between the dot and the fold for the nose.

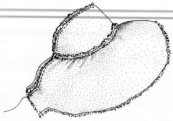

12 Right sides together, pin the head front to the head back. Stitch.

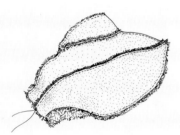

13 Install the safety eyes as instructed on page 46.

14 Turn head right side out. Insert the head, turned upside down, into the body. Pin the neck edge of the head to the neck edge of the body, easing the head to fit. Stitch. Turn the bear right side out.

15 Right sides together, stitch one ear piece of each color fur together along the curved edges. Turn right side out. Repeat for the remaining ear.

16 Trim the nose covering piece into a rounded triangular shape.

Using a tiny seam allowance, about $1/8$-inch (3mm), baste around the edge of the nose covering piece. With the wrong side of the fabric against the nose, place the fabric covering on the nose. Pull up on the threads to gather the fabric around the back of the nose. Stitch back and forth to secure. As instructed for safety eyes on page 46, install the nose in the opening left in the stitching in the muzzle.

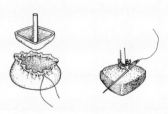

17 Stuff the bear.

18 Stitch the opening at the back of the body closed (see page 17).

19 Stitch the ears to the head.

Stuffing Basics

As with most skills, stuffing is a learned art. For the best results don't economize; use high quality stuffing since inferior products tend to lump in the bear. "Bargain" brands often have highly visible clumps of strands which are easily seen when you inspect a bag. The long polyester fibers of quality fiberfill stuffing make the bag appear perfectly uniform upon inspection. It is resilient and will remain uniform in texture, even after pieces of various sizes are stuffed into the bear. High quality stuffing costs a bit more, but it is a small price to pay for an easily and evenly stuffed bear.

Stuffing tools will make the job easier as well. The handle of a wooden spoon serves splendidly as a bear stuffing tool. The Stuff-It® tool, a chopstick, or a dowel can also be used for stuffing bears.

Begin by stuffing the smallest areas, and those farthest from the opening first. For noses, use pieces of fiberfill about the size of a walnut. Pack each piece in firmly before adding another. A stuffing tool aids greatly here. Stuffing tends to migrate from noses and paws unless packed in firmly. For the body, use large handfuls of stuffing.

Check your bear as you stuff to make sure the stuffing is even. Are the arms both stuffed equally, or is one stuffed harder or fatter? Are there any lumps? Is the nose firm or will it cave in when I poke my needle in to embroider the nose? Take the time to unstuff and correct these problems now.

Use your hands to sculpt the bear as you stuff. Make a paw bend or indent the eye area by squeezing the stuffed bear.

With practice, your skill will improve and stuffing will be faster.

Stuffing with Plastic Pellets

Plastic pellets give a bear weight and make it poseable. Pellets are easy to use, though you should take care when filling your bear as spilled pellets can create a bit of a mess.

When using pellets, stuff the paws and nose with fiberfill as usual. Insert a funnel into the bear and scoop the pellets through the funnel into the bear. Fill the bear with pellets. Insert pieces of fiberfill to cover the pellets at the opening in the body part. Ladderstitch the opening closed.

clothing

materials

Dress
* ⅓ yard (30.5cm) of fabric
* Matching thread
* 1 yard (91.5cm) of ¼-inch (6mm) -wide ribbon

Jumper
* ⅓ yard (30.5cm) of fabric
* Matching thread
* Two ⅜-inch (1cm) buttons

Shorts
* ¼ yard (22.8cm) of fabric
* Matching thread
* ¼ yard (22.8cm) of ¼-inch (6mm) -wide elastic

Vest
* ¼ yard (22.8cm) fabric for vest and lining
* Matching thread
* Three ½-inch (1.2cm) buttons

Bow Tie
* ⅛ yard (11.4cm) fabric
* Matching thread
* ¼ yard (22.8cm) ⅜-inch (1cm) -wide black elastic

instructions

Note: All seam allowances are ¼ inch (6mm) unless otherwise noted.

Prepare all patterns and fabric as instructed on pages 12 and 13.

Dress

1 Make a buttonhole at the center front of the dress as marked. This will allow the ribbon to come through the casing at the neck edge.

2 Right sides together, match the long edges of the dress body pieces. Stitch both sides from the neck edge to the top dot, and from the bottom dot to the hem edge.

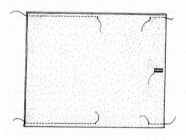

3 Press ¼ inch then 1¼ inches (6mm then 3.2cm) at the raw edge at the top of the dress to the wrong side. Topstitch close to the bottom fold and again ⅜ inch (1cm) away.

4 Press ¼ inch (6mm) at the remaining raw hem edge to the wrong side twice. Topstitch.

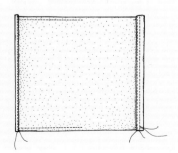

5 Make buttonholes at the markings on the two sleeves.

6 Fold one sleeve in half so the underarm edges meet. Stitch the underarm seam. Repeat for the second sleeve.

7 Press ¼ inch then 1¼ inches (6mm then 3.2cm) at the hem (buttonhole) edge of the sleeve to the wrong side. Topstitch close to the last fold and again ⅜ inch (1cm) away, as shown.

8 Stitch the remaining raw edge of the sleeve to the armhole in the side seam of the dress. Pin and stitch one half to the front of the dress, and then the other half to the back of the dress. Turn dress right side out.

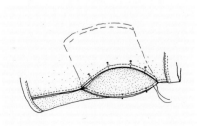

Jumper

1 Right sides together, seam the two jumper pieces at the side seams. Repeat for the two jumper lining pieces.

2 With right sides together and matching the raw edges, pin and stitch the jumper lining to the jumper at the neck and armhole edges. Turn right side out. Press.

3 Press ¹/4 inch (6mm) to the wrong side twice at the hem edge of the jumper. Topstitch. Do the same for the jumper lining.

4 Make buttonholes at the markings on the front tabs of the jumper. Sew buttons at the markings on the back tabs of the jumper.

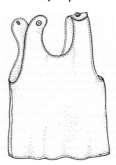

Shorts

1 With right sides together and matching inseam, fold one shorts piece in half. Stitch inseam. Repeat for other shorts piece.

2 Turn one shorts piece right side out. Slip inside second shorts piece, matching the raw edges at the crotch. Stitch the crotch seam. Turn right side out.

3 Press ¹/4 inch (6mm) to the wrong side twice along the bottom edge of each pants leg. Topstitch.

4 Press ¹/4 inch then ¹/2 inch (6mm then 1.2cm) to the wrong side at the top edge of the shorts. Topstitch close to the top and bottom folds, leaving a ¹/2-inch (1.2cm) -wide opening in the stitching for inserting the elastic in the casing.

9 Put the dress on the bear. Attach a safety pin to one end of the ribbon. Insert the pin into the buttonhole at the neck edge of the dress. Pull the safety pin through the casing and out the buttonhole again. Pull up on the ribbon to gather the dress around the bear's neck. Tie the ribbon into a bow, and trim ends. Repeat for the two sleeves.

5 Attach a safety pin to one end of the elastic. Insert the safety pin into the opening, through the casing, and out the opening.

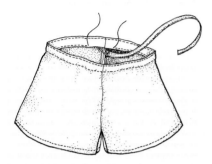

6 Put the shorts on the bear. Pull up the elastic to fit. Pin. Stitch the elastic ends together. Topstitch the opening in the casing closed.

Vest

1 With right sides facing, stitch two back pieces to two front pieces at shoulders. Repeat with the remaining set to make the lining.

2 Right sides together, match and pin the vest and vest lining. Stitch leaving the side seams open and an opening at the bottom back edge for turning. Turn right side out. Press.

3 Whipstitch the side seams closed. Stitch the opening at the bottom back closed.

4 Make buttonholes at the markings. Try vest on bear. Sew buttons in place.

Bow tie

1 For the bow, cut a piece of fabric 3 × 8 inches (7.6 × 20.5cm). For the tie, cut a piece 1¹/₂ × 3 inches (3.8 × 7.6cm).

2 Right sides facing, stitch the three raw edges of the bow, leaving a 1-inch (2.5cm) opening at the center for turning. Turn right side out.

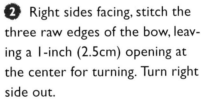

3 Fold the bow as shown, overlapping the ends. Pinch the center. Fold the raw edges of the tie to the wrong side. Wrap around the center of the bow. Fold the raw

edges of the tie to the wrong side. Tack securely, securing the pinch in the tie.

4 Put the elastic around the bear's neck. Overlap the ends ¹/₂ inch (1.2cm), then trim. Remove from the bear. Stitch the ends of the elastic together. Stitch the back of the bow tie to the elastic.

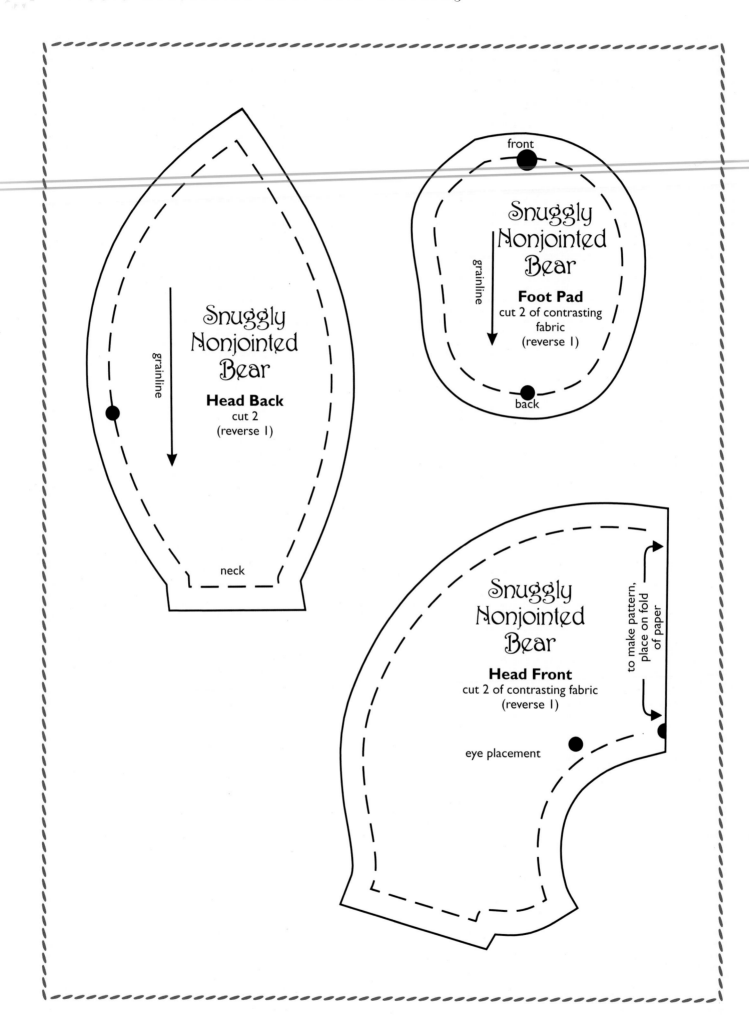

Snuggly Nonjointed Bear

Head Back
cut 2
(reverse 1)

grainline

neck

Snuggly Nonjointed Bear

Foot Pad
cut 2 of contrasting fabric
(reverse 1)

front

back

grainline

Snuggly Nonjointed Bear

Head Front
cut 2 of contrasting fabric
(reverse 1)

eye placement

to make pattern, place on fold of paper

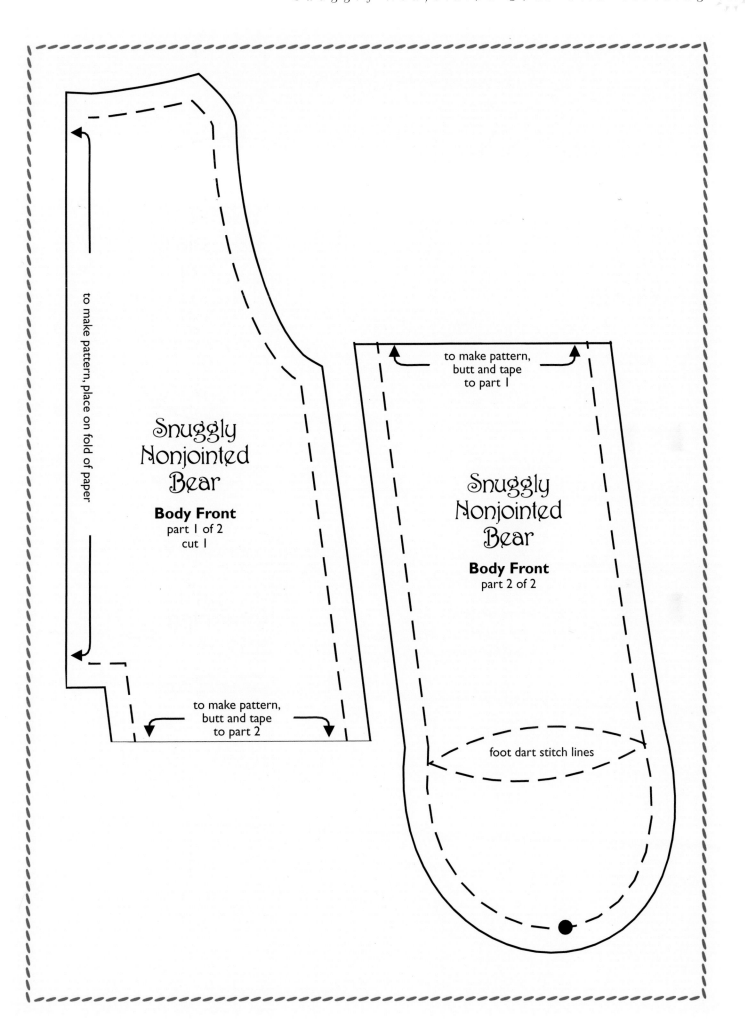

to make pattern, place on fold of paper

Snuggly
Nonjointed
Bear

Body Front
part 1 of 2
cut 1

to make pattern,
butt and tape
to part 2

to make pattern,
butt and tape
to part 1

Snuggly
Nonjointed
Bear

Body Front
part 2 of 2

foot dart stitch lines

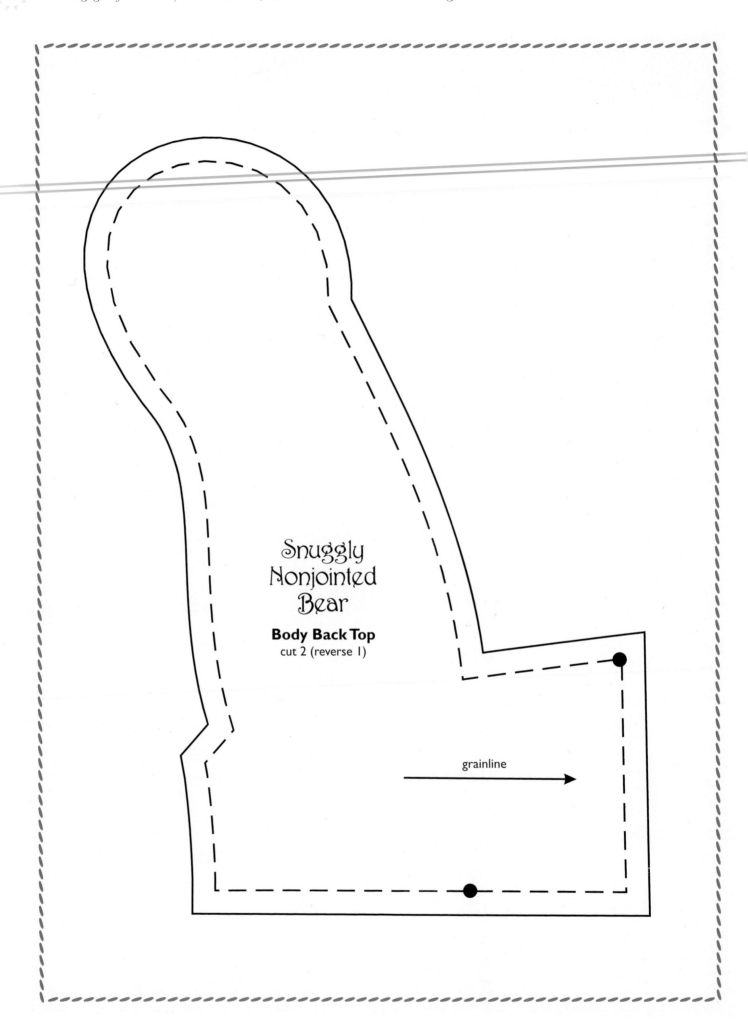

Snuggly
Nonjointed
Bear

Body Back Top
cut 2 (reverse 1)

grainline

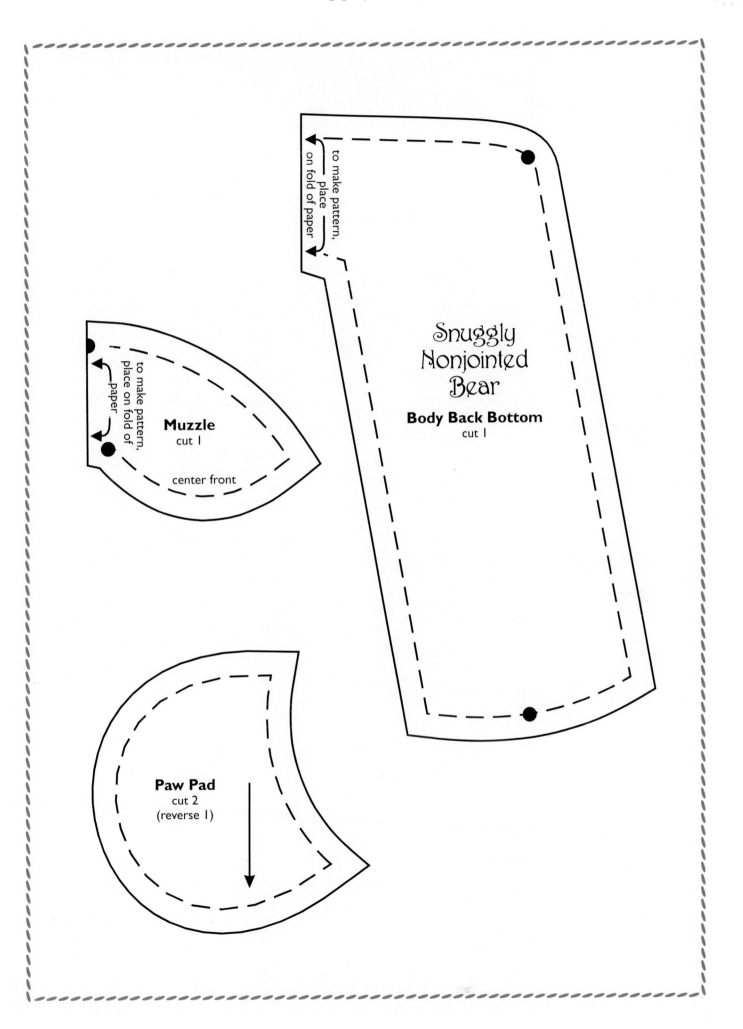

Muzzle
cut 1

to make pattern, place on fold of paper

center front

Snuggly
Nonjointed
Bear

Body Back Bottom
cut 1

to make pattern, place on fold of paper

Paw Pad
cut 2
(reverse 1)

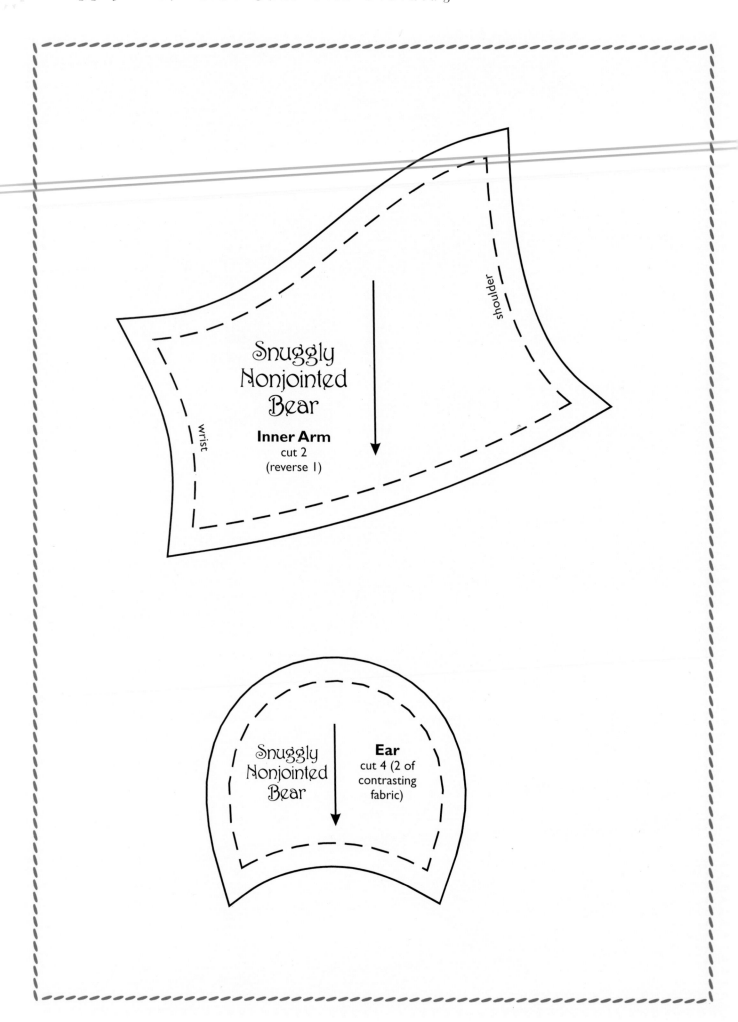

Snuggly
Nonjointed
Bear

Inner Arm
cut 2
(reverse 1)

shoulder

wrist

Snuggly
Nonjointed
Bear

Ear
cut 4 (2 of
contrasting
fabric)

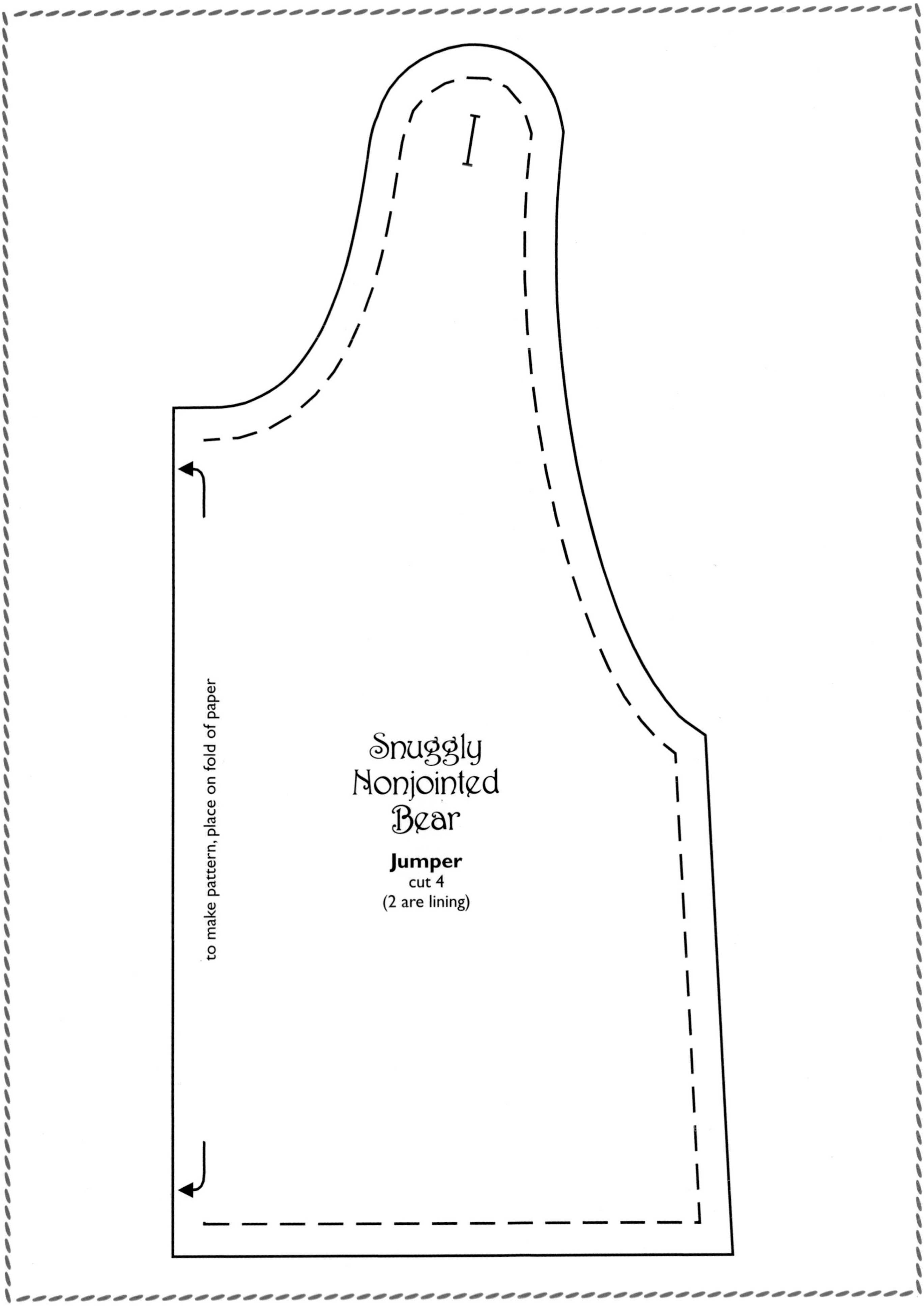

I

to make pattern, place on fold of paper

Snuggly Nonjointed Bear

Jumper
cut 4
(2 are lining)

armhole

Snuggly Nonjointed Bear

Dress
cut 2

(transfer buttonhole and
armhole dots to top half only)

neck edge

to make pattern, place on fold of paper

armhole

chapter four

Classic Jointed Bear with Clothing

Finished size: 20 inches (50.8cm)

I designed this bear to look like the bear we picture when we hear the magical name "teddy bear." With a large, wide head, ample tummy, and a hump in its back, this bear's proportions make it a classic. ❀ Since this is our first foray into jointing bears, a full discussion of the jointing method as well as alternative jointing mechanisms is included. ❀ You will also find a clothing pattern for a sundress. ❀ For a variation, I present a quilted bear. Rather than use an old quilt as fabric for the bear, I've included complete instructions for foundation piecing the bear's body parts. This simple technique uses a marked fabric as a base on which to stitch the patchwork pieces. The technique is super-easy and guarantees excellent results—even for a beginner.

materials

For fur bear

* ¹/₂ yard (45.7cm) of synthetic fur fabric
* Small piece of suede or wool felt for paw pads and soles

For patchwork bear

* 18-inch (45.7cm) -square piece of fur fabric
* ⁵/₈ yard (57cm) of muslin
* ⁵/₈ yard (57cm) of fusible fleece
* ¹/₄ yard (22.8cm) each of five cotton print fabrics

For either bear

* **Matching thread**
* **Five sets of 2¹/₂-inch (6.3cm) joints**
* **Two 16mm eyes**
* **Waxed dental floss or carpet thread**
* **Polyester fiberfill stuffing**
* **Perle cotton or embroidery floss**

instructions

Note: All seam allowances are ¹/₄ inch (6mm).

❶ Prepare the patterns and cut out the fur as instructed on pages 12 and 13.

❷ With right sides together, pin the two body fronts along the center front seam. Stitch.

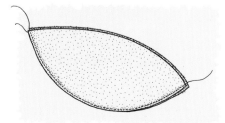

❸ With right sides together, pin the two body backs along the center back seam. Stitch the seam from the top to the first dot, then from the second dot to the bottom. The opening left in the stitching between the two dots will provide access to the body for jointing and stuffing the bear.

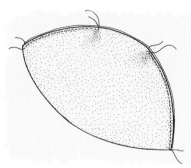

❹ With right sides together, pin the front left side to the back left side and the front right side to the back right side. Stitch the sides from the front dots down, leaving a small opening between the dots at the top to allow room for a neck joint. Turn the body right side out.

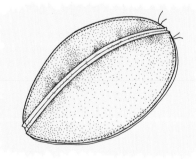

❺ Right sides together, pin paw pads to inner arms. Stitch.

❻ Right sides together and with the paw pads opened, pin the outer arms to the inner arms. Stitch around the arm, leaving an opening between the dots at the top of the arm for turning and stuffing. Turn the arms right side out.

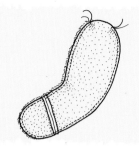

❼ With right sides together, pin the pairs of legs together. Stitch from the dot at the front of the thigh down the leg ending at the foot. Stitch from the dot at the back of the thigh down to the foot.

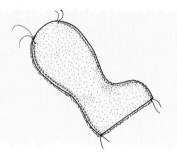

❽ With right sides together, pin the foot pads to the bottom of the feet. Match the large dot on the foot pad to the front leg seam and the small dot to the back leg seam. Stitch, having the foot pad against the sewing machine bed. Turn the legs right side out.

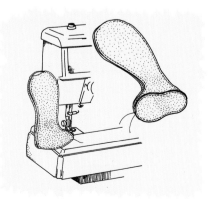

9 With right sides together, pin the two side head pieces. Stitch from the nose to the base of the neck.

10 Pin the dot on the gusset to the seam where the two head pieces meet at the tip of the nose. Pin one side of the gusset from the tip of the nose to the base of the neck, easing the gusset to fit as you go. Stitch.

Repeat for the other side. Turn the head right side out.

Jointing Bears

Installation of joints will allow your bear to turn its head and move its arms, and offers the option of a sitting or standing bear.

Following are step-by-step instructions for jointing a bear using traditional hardboard disks, washers, and cotter pins. Sometimes called "crown joints," cotter pin joints require strength to achieve the necessary tightness. For this reason, bear makers have devised several alternative jointing mechanisms. These include plastic doll joints with the addition of a metal lock washer, bolts and locknuts used with hardboard disks, and pop rivets, also used in conjunction with hardboard disks. Each option is fully explained following the cotter pin instructions.

1. To joint the bear, begin with the stuffed head. Place a washer and then a hardboard disk on a cotter pin. Push the cotter pin, washer side first, into the head opening. Thread a needle with dental floss or heavy thread. Make a knot at one end. Baste $1/4$-inch (6mm) seam allowance around the neck opening. Pull up on the thread to gather the neck. Stitch around again, pulling up on the thread every few stitches. Continue until the fabric is closed around the cotter pin.

2. If using glass eyes, install them now as instructed on page 46.

3. Push the cotter pin protruding from the bottom of the head through the small opening in the stitching at the top of the body and into the body cavity. Slip a disk and then a washer over the cotter pin. Check to be sure that no extra fabric is caught between the disks.

With the needlenose pliers, bend the cotter pin. To ensure a tight joint, hold the washer on the disk with (if you are right-handed) your left thumb as

you tighten the cotter pin to keep it flat on the disk. Check the tightness of the joint and tighten again if needed.

4. With a small scissors, an awl, or a seam ripper, carefully make holes for the joints on the inside arms as marked. Hold the legs together, toes pointing in the same direction. Make a hole at the joint placement mark on the inside of each of the legs.

5. Put a washer and then a hardboard disk on a cotter pin. Insert the cotter pins through the holes you made for them in the arms and legs so that the post is protruding from the limb.

6. Make holes for the arms and legs at the marked points on the body. Install the arms and legs on the body as you did the head. Double check the direction of the limbs—taking apart a completed bear is no fun! Get the joints tight; they loosen up over time.

Pop Rivets

Favored by many bear makers, pop rivets create a tight joint and require little strength on the part of the bear maker. A pop rivet tool, available at most hardware stores, makes installation of the pop rivet easy. The rivets are used with two hardboard disks and two washers, all of which are available from suppliers listed in the Sources section (see page 124). Follow the instructions provided with the rivet tool.

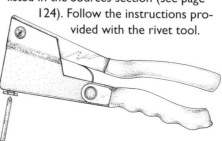

Plastic Joints

Plastic doll joints are another jointing option. These have the advantage of being widely available (most crafts stores carry them), inexpensive, lightweight, and easy to install. Their disadvantage is that they are not the strongest available joints.

This shortcoming can be partially compensated for by the addition of a metal lock washer as a fourth piece of the joint.

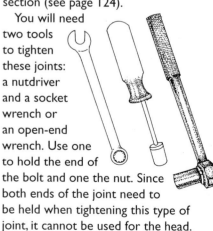

To get the joint as tight as possible, use a little elbow grease and a hammer. Install the joint as in the diagram. Put a socket from a ratchet set, or two large metal washers (two stacked are tall enough to clear the post), over the post. Pound with the hammer. The joint should be too difficult to turn. Now add the metal lock washer. To obtain the lock washer, you will have to buy the right size along with a pair of safety eyes, then discard the eyes.

Bolt and Locknut

A fourth type of joint uses a bolt and locknut along with the hardboard disks. Many professional bear makers prefer this method. The supplies are available from suppliers listed in the Sources section (see page 124).

You will need two tools to tighten these joints: a nutdriver and a socket wrench or an open-end wrench. Use one to hold the end of the bolt and one the nut. Since both ends of the joint need to be held when tightening this type of joint, it cannot be used for the head.

Eyes

Many antique bears' eyes were made from real shoe buttons. Black and shiny, these made perfect bear eyes. Though stashes of old shoe buttons are often available to bear makers today, most contemporary bears sport either safety eyes or glass eyes.

Safety eyes are easy to install and are the only choice for bears intended for children as these eyes are sure to stay put. Safety eyes are available in traditional solid black or a realistic dark translucent brown with a black pupil.

Glass eyes are handmade, shiny, and have a lifelike quality to them. Usually offered as a pair, one on each end of a wire, glass eyes vary slightly in size, shape, and placement of the pupil because they are handmade. For this reason, it is advisable to have several pairs from which to choose individual eyes to get a good match.

Safety eyes are installed before the head is stuffed, glass eyes after.

In addition to these choices, bear makers use a variety of buttons for bear eyes, and for small bears, beads are often just the right size.

I have not included eye placement markings for most of the bears. I find slight variations in sewing and stuffing often cause inaccuracies. In addition, my students enjoy deciding the personality of their bears, of which eyes are an important factor.

Installing Safety Eyes

1. Make a hole in the fur with an awl. Smooth the fibers away from the hole. From the right side of the fur, poke the shaft of the eye into the hole.

2. Put the eye right side down on a padded surface to avoid scratching the eye. From inside the head, place the washer on the shaft of the eye, teeth up. Push the washer down the shaft, using a thumb on each side. Standing and leaning onto your thumbs will help snap the washer into place. An alternative is to slip a large spool onto the shaft and force the washer down with the palm of your hand.

Installing Glass Eyes

1. If you are using prelooped glass eyes, go on to the next step. Otherwise, use wire cutters to cut the wire about $^3/_4$ inch (1.8cm) from each eye. Bend the last third of the wire back on itself and down again.

2. Experiment with eye positions by pushing two pins into the head and repositioning them until you are happy with their placement. With small scissors, an awl, (or my favorite, though you must be careful) a seam ripper, make holes at the pins for the eyes. Double

thread a long dollmaker's needle with heavy thread. Push the needle through the bottom of the bear's head and come out of the fur at the edge of the disk between the front and one side of the bear. Pull on the thread very tightly. Go back into the base of the neck close to where you just came out, emerging through the eyehole.

It may take a few stabs to get the needle to come out exactly in the hole.

3. Put the needle through the loop in the eye wire (or, if the needle is too large for the hole in the loop, just work the thread onto the loop as you would as if linking one paper clip to another) and push the needle back into the head.

4. Push the needle out through the base of the neck near where you pushed it in before coming out at the eye. Pull the thread very tightly, seating the eye flatly and firmly against the head. Pull again to be sure the eye is secure and loop is inside the head.

5. Take a stitch in the fabric covering the disk to secure the thread. Take another stitch, emerging on the edge of the disk between the other side and front of the head. Push the needle back in close to where it came out, emerging through the second eyehole. Continue as above taking a stitch at the base of the neck to secure the thread, and being sure both eyes are tight before knotting the thread.

Note: Glass eyes and button or bead eyes should not be used on bears intended for small children.

11 With right sides together, pin and sew the rounded edge of the ears, leaving the lower edge open. Turn. Turn seam allowance to the wrong side along lower edge. Whipstitch closed.

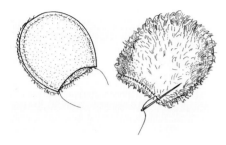

12 If using safety eyes, install them now as instructed on page 46.

13 To stuff the head, begin with the nose, pushing table tennis ball–size pieces of fiberfill firmly into place with a stuffing tool. Continue with larger pieces of stuffing until the head is firmly stuffed to within about $^3/_4$ inch (1.8cm) of the neck opening. Check to be sure the stuffing is even, restuffing if necessary.

14 Stuff the body, arms, and legs. Stitch the openings closed using a ladderstitch as instructed on page 17.

15 Decide where you want the ears. Pin them in place. Stitch them to the head in a circular motion, sewing through the ear at the top of the circle and the head on the bottom of the circle.

16 Embroider the nose and mouth, following the instructions on page 75.

foundation pieced patchwork bear

1 Trace the body arm and leg patterns onto the muslin, leaving about 2 inches (5cm) between the pattern pieces. Transfer the markings to the fabric with dressmaker's carbon paper. Transfer all pattern markings as well.

2 Fuse the fusible fleece to the unmarked side of the muslin. Cut out the pattern pieces, about 1 inch (2.5cm) outside the pattern lines.

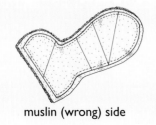

muslin (wrong) side

Note: You will be stitching from the wrong side of the fabric, which is the marked side of the muslin.

3 Cut two pieces of patchwork fabric, one for piece 1 and one for piece 2, cutting them larger than the marked pieces. Place patchwork piece 1 right side up on the fusible fleece so it covers the section marked 1 on the muslin. Pin.

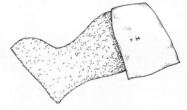

fleece (right) side

4 Place patchwork piece 2 over piece 1, so right sides are together. Stitch along the seamline between piece 1 and piece 2. Extend the stitching 1/4 inch (6mm) or more beyond the ends of the marked seamline.

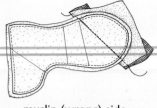

muslin (wrong) side

5 Trim the seam allowances to about 1/4 inch (6mm).

6 Open up piece 2 and finger press into position.

fleece (right) side

7 Add piece 3 and so on.

8 When the piecing is complete, baste just outside the stitching line. Trim all layers along the solid outside cutting line.

9 Repeat for all body, arm, and leg pieces. Make the paw and foot pads from solid fabric. Make the head from fur fabric. Assemble the bear as instructed on pages 42–47.

sundress

materials

Sundress
* $1/3$ yard (30.5cm) of fabric
* Matching thread
* Two $5/8$-inch (1.5cm) buttons

Overalls
* $1/3$ yard (30.5cm) of fabric
* Matching thread
* Two $5/8$-inch (1.5cm) buttons

instructions

1 Prepare the patterns and cut out fabric as instructed on pages 12 and 13. Cut a 3 × 20-inch (7.6 × 50.8cm) waistband and two $2^1/2$ × 12-inch (6.3 × 30.5cm) straps. Cut a $7^1/2$ × 22-inch (19 × 55.9cm) skirt.

2 Right sides together, fold skirt so the short edges match. Stitch.

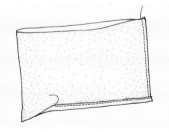

3 Press $1/4$ inch (6mm) twice to the wrong side on the bottom of one raw edge of the skirt. Topstitch.

4 Right sides together, stitch the short ends of the waistband together. Gather the remaining raw edge of the skirt. Pin waistband to raw edge, right sides together. Adjust gathers to fit. Stitch.

5 Fold waistband to inside. Turn raw edge $1/4$ inch (6mm) to inside. Topstitch.

6 Right sides together, fold straps in half lengthwise. Stitch across one short end and the long edge. Turn right side out. Stitch to back of skirt. Sew to front with button.

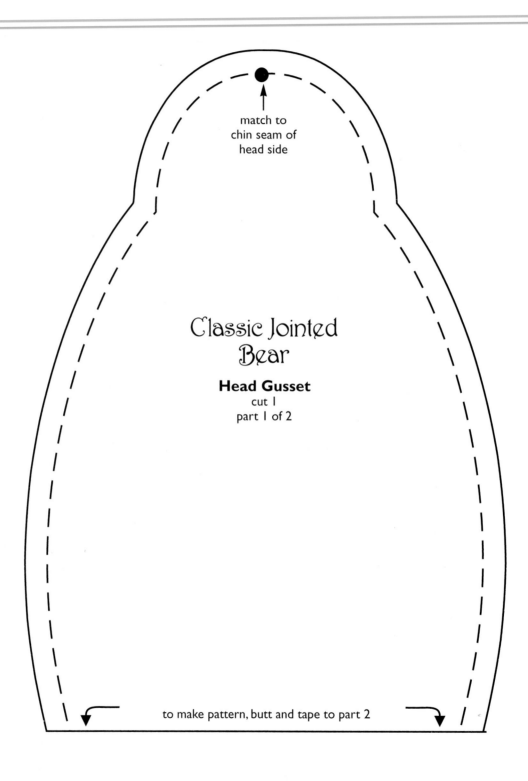

match to
chin seam of
head side

Classic Jointed
Bear

Head Gusset
cut 1
part 1 of 2

to make pattern, butt and tape to part 2

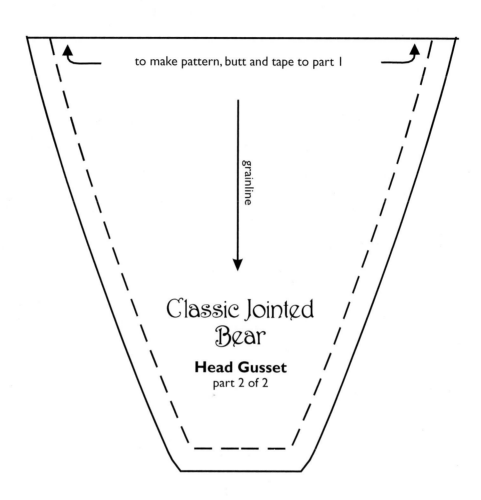

to make pattern, butt and tape to part 1

grainline

Classic Jointed Bear

Head Gusset
part 2 of 2

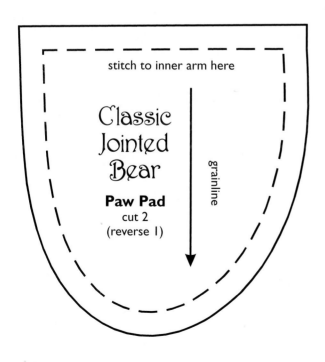

stitch to inner arm here

grainline

Classic Jointed Bear

Paw Pad
cut 2
(reverse 1)

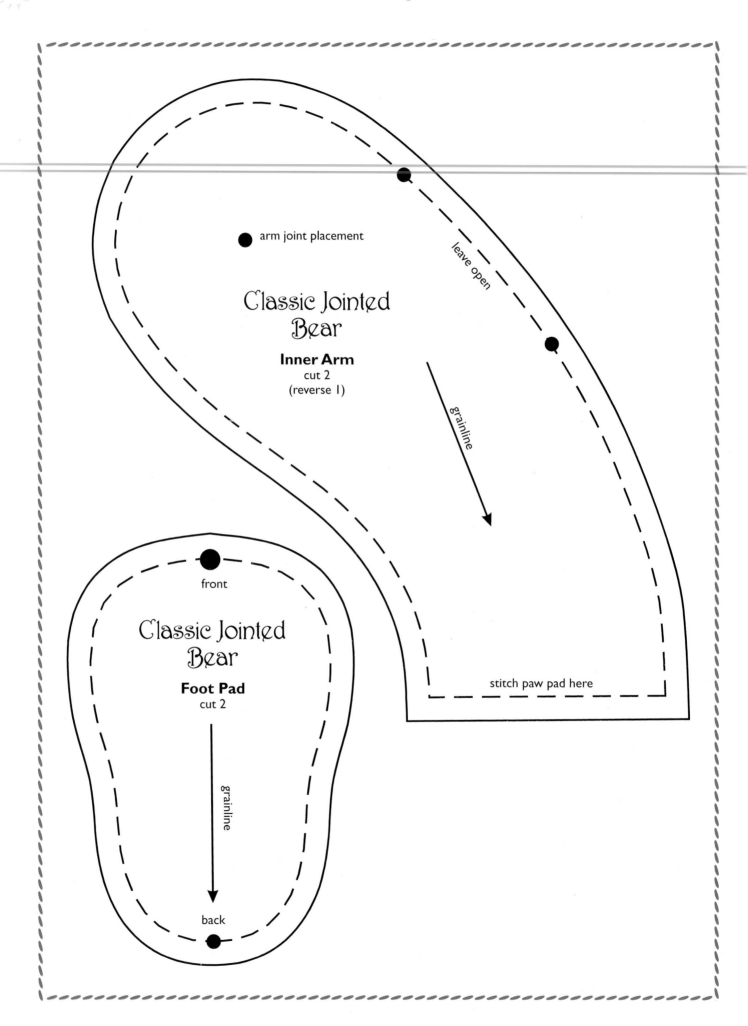

arm joint placement

Classic Jointed Bear

Inner Arm
cut 2
(reverse 1)

leave open

grainline

stitch paw pad here

front

Classic Jointed Bear

Foot Pad
cut 2

grainline

back

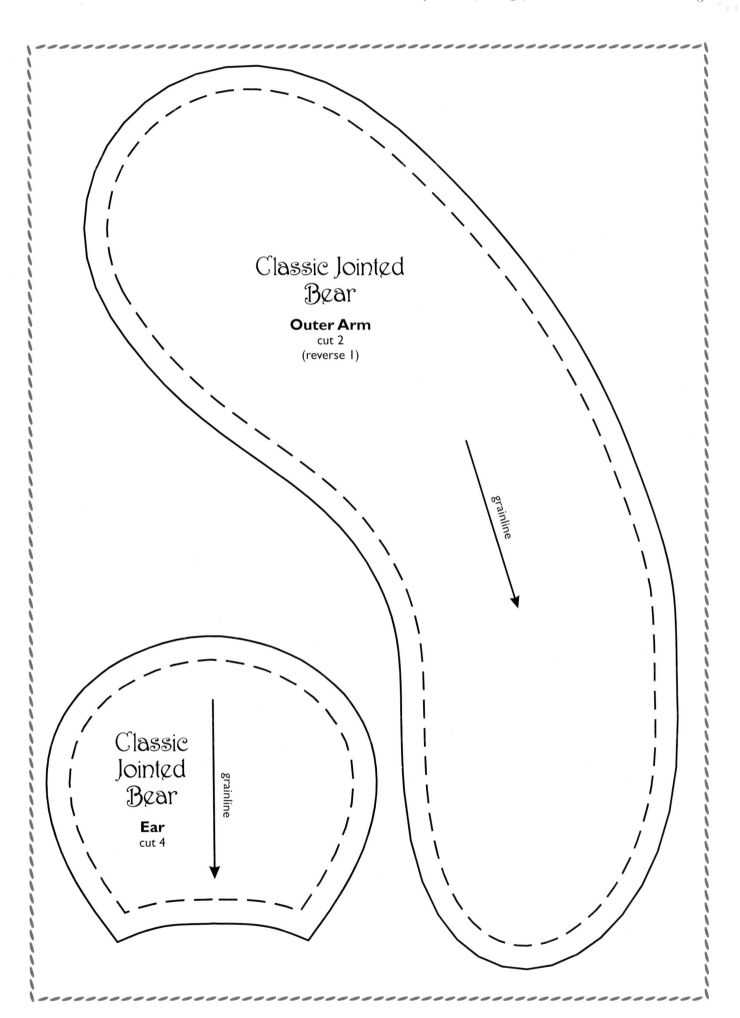

Classic Jointed
Bear

Outer Arm
cut 2
(reverse 1)

grainline

Classic
Jointed
Bear

Ear
cut 4

grainline

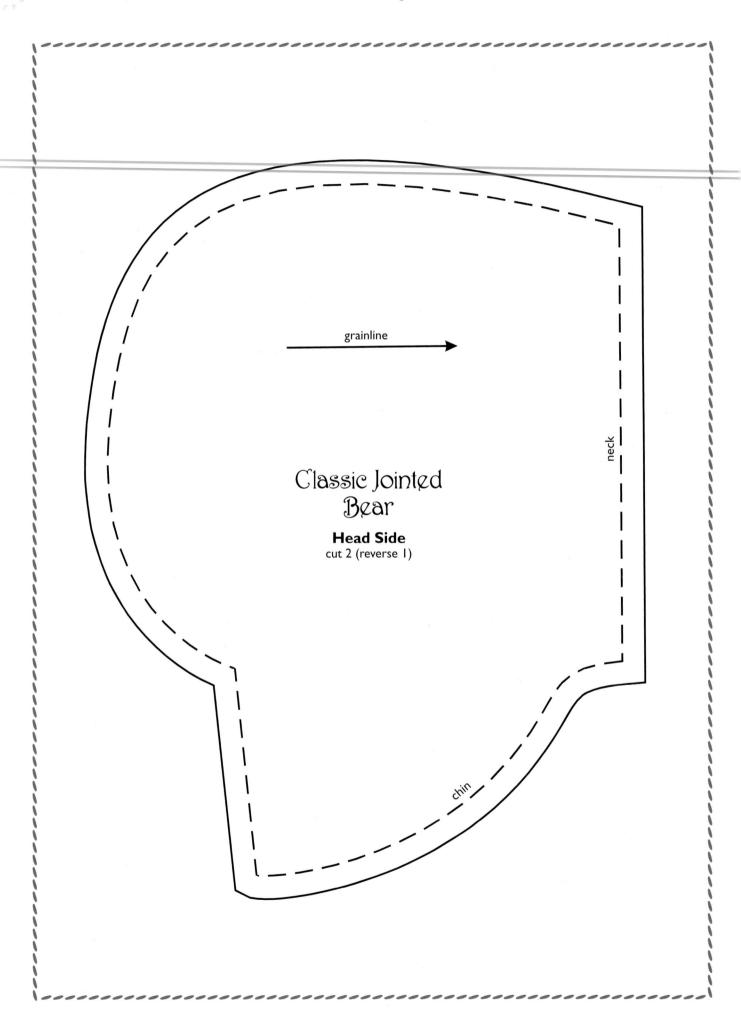

grainline

neck

Classic Jointed Bear

Head Side
cut 2 (reverse 1)

chin

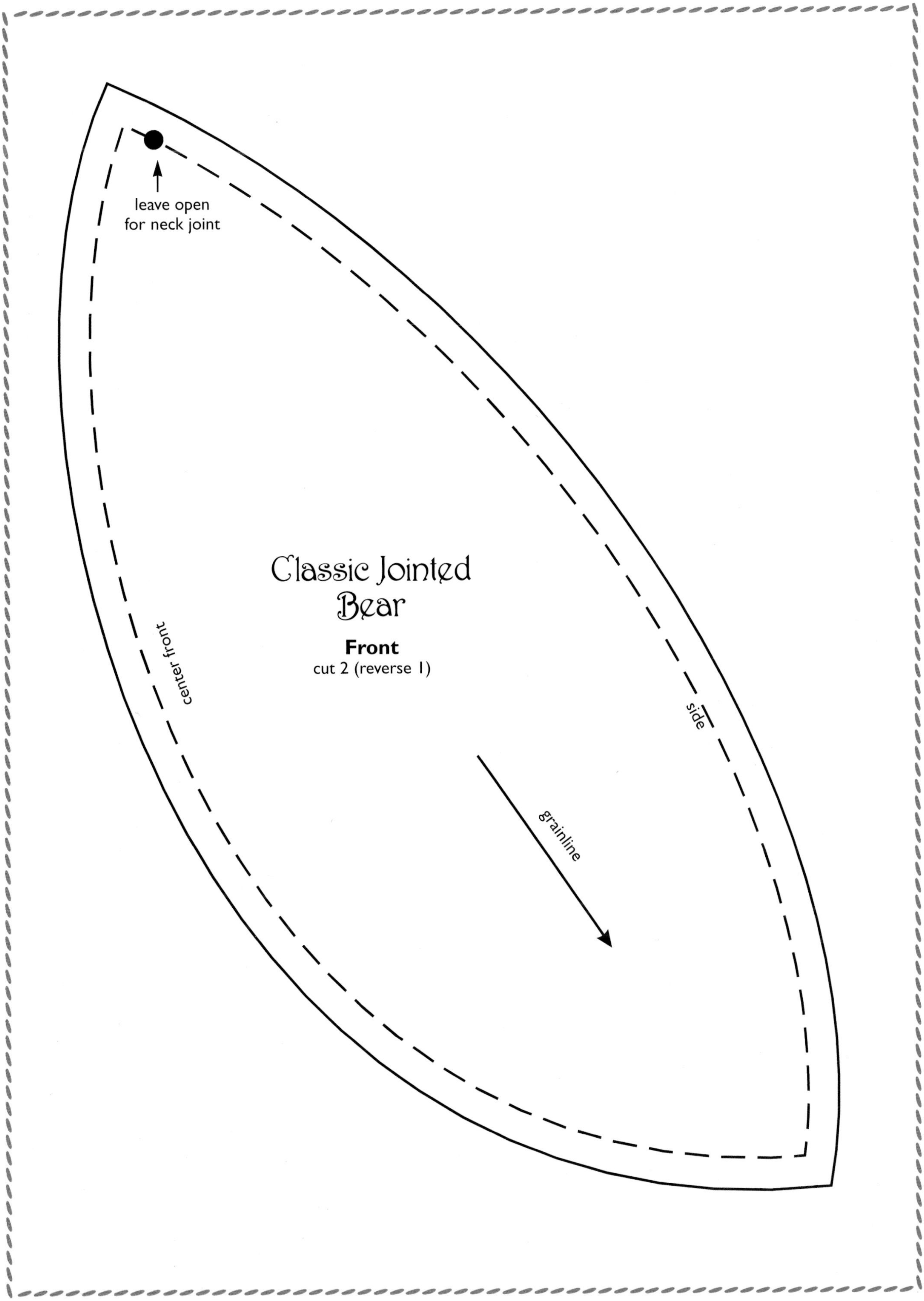

leave open
for neck joint

Classic Jointed
Bear

Front
cut 2 (reverse 1)

center front

side

grainline

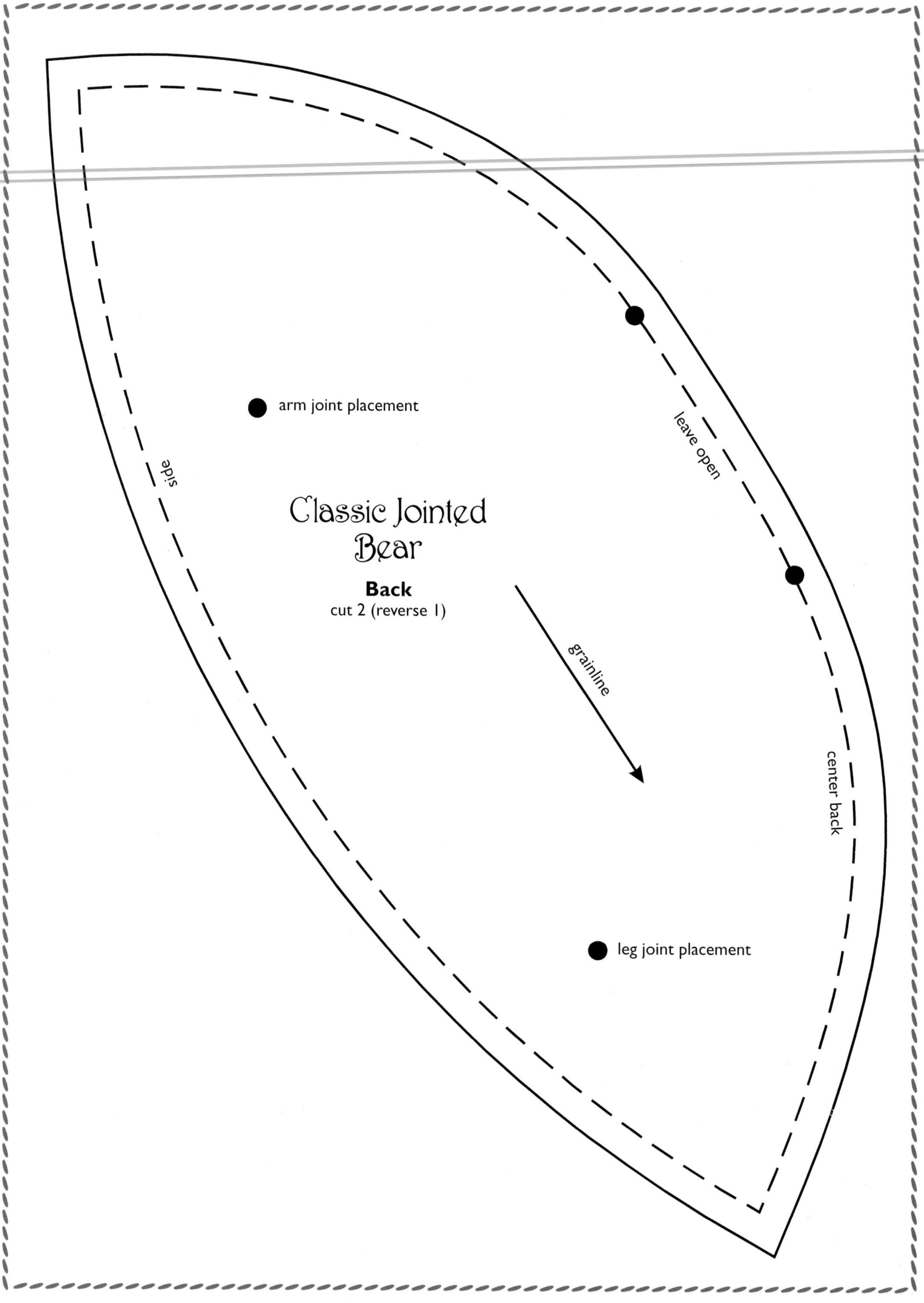

side

arm joint placement

leave open

Classic Jointed Bear

Back
cut 2 (reverse 1)

grainline

center back

leg joint placement

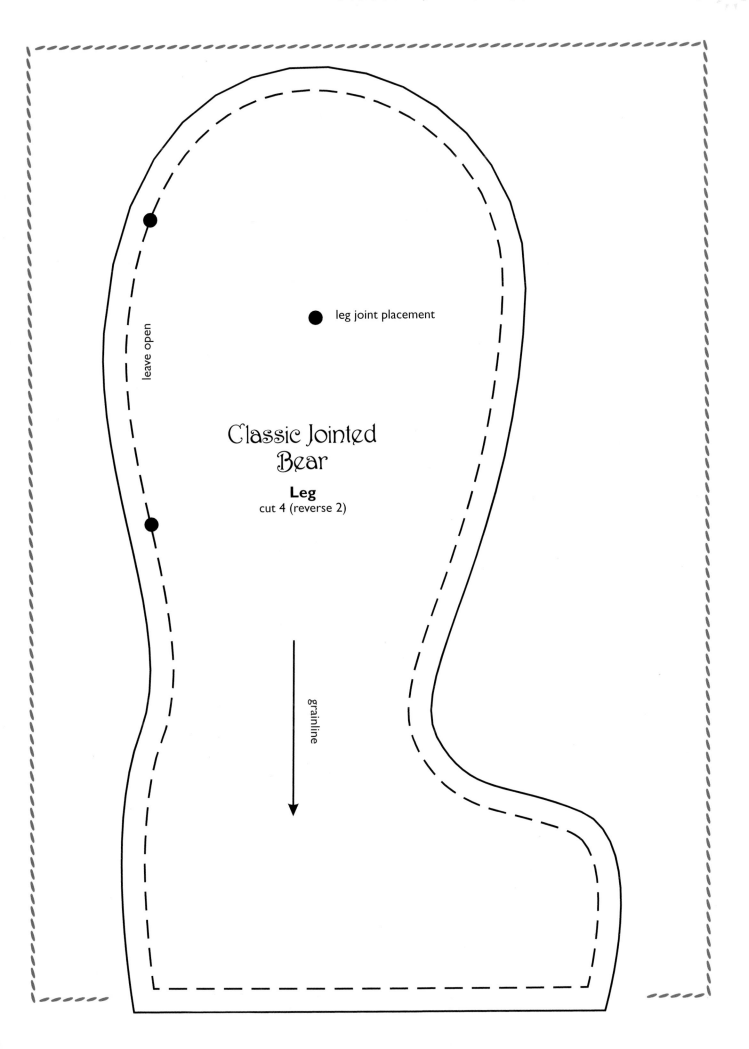

leg joint placement

leave open

Classic Jointed
Bear

Leg
cut 4 (reverse 2)

grainline

**For cutting
see instructions**

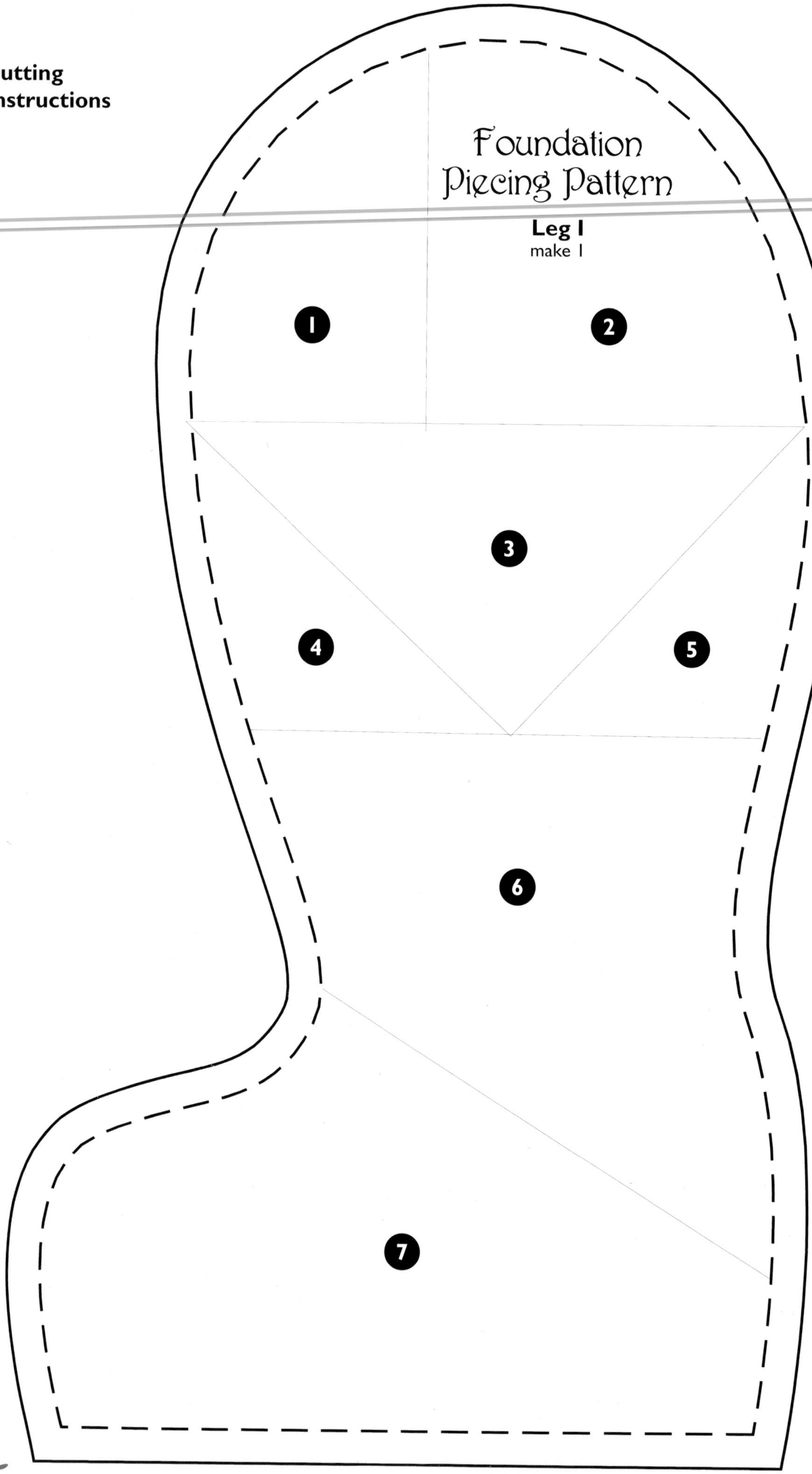

Foundation
Piecing Pattern

Leg I
make I

1

2

3

4

5

6

7

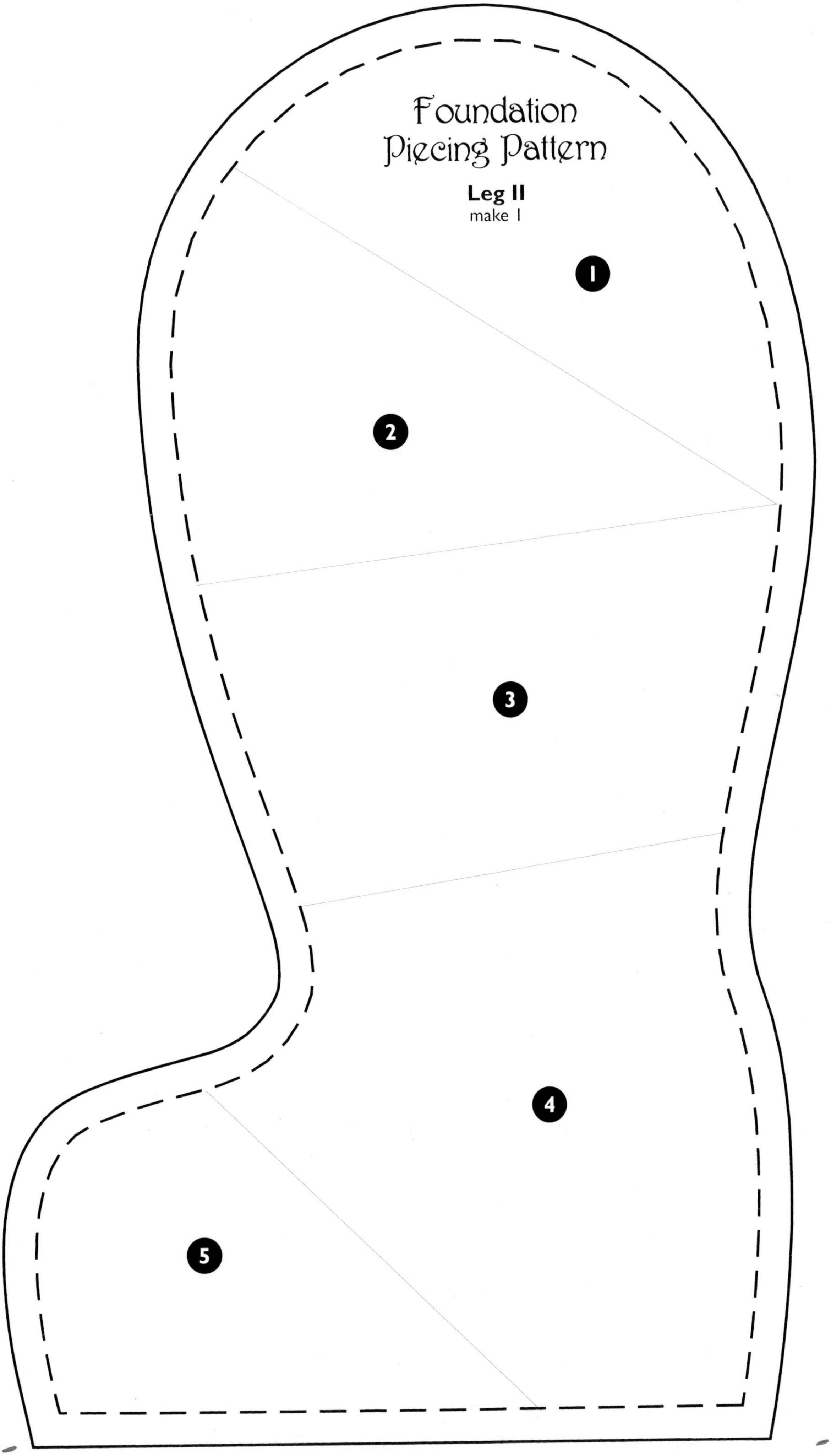

Foundation
Piecing Pattern

Leg II
make 1

1

2

3

4

5

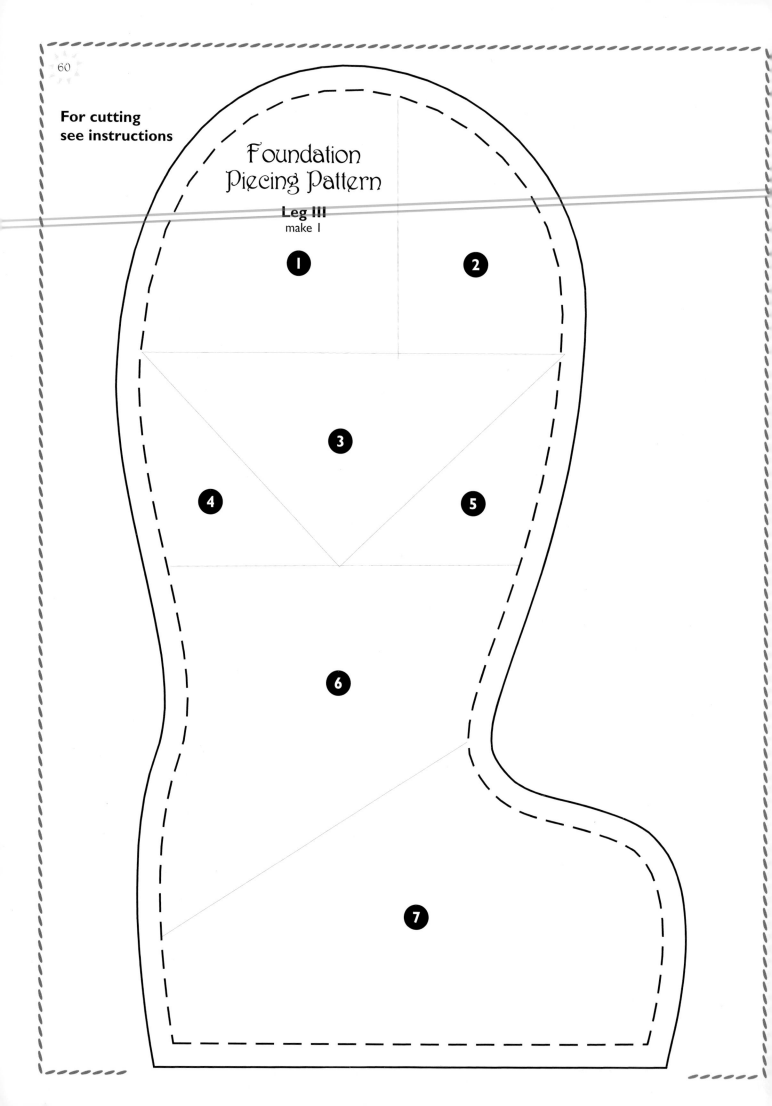

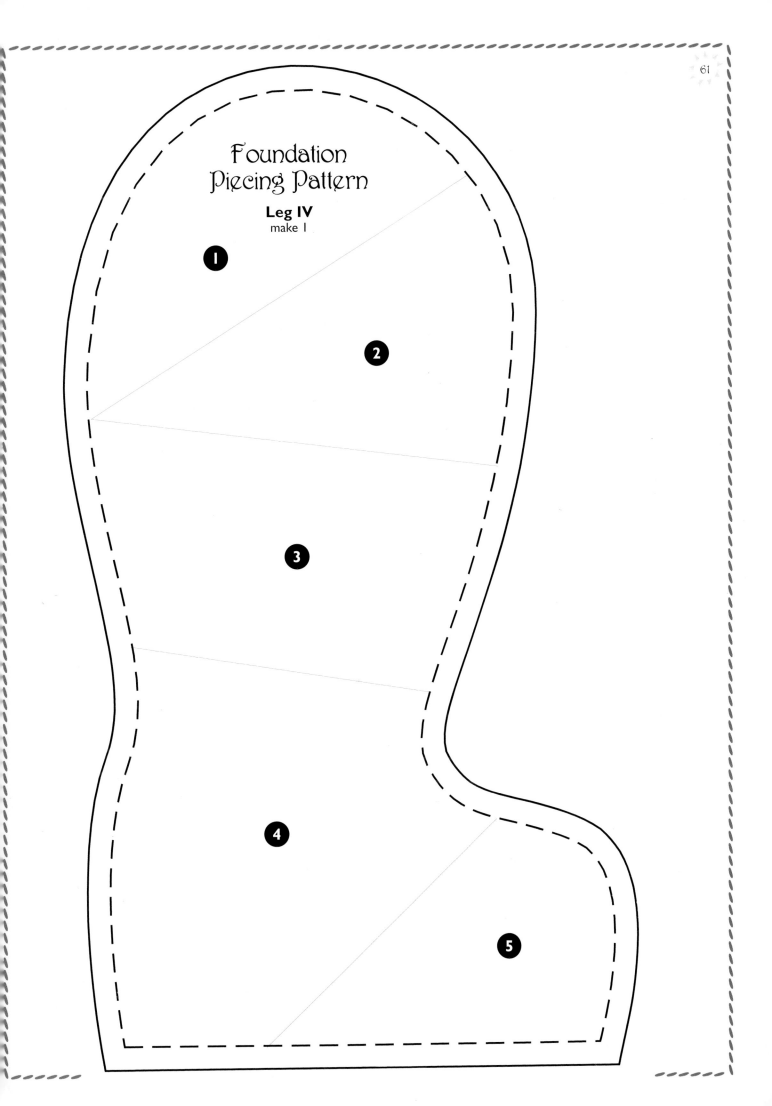

Foundation
Piecing Pattern

Leg IV
make 1

1

2

3

4

5

61

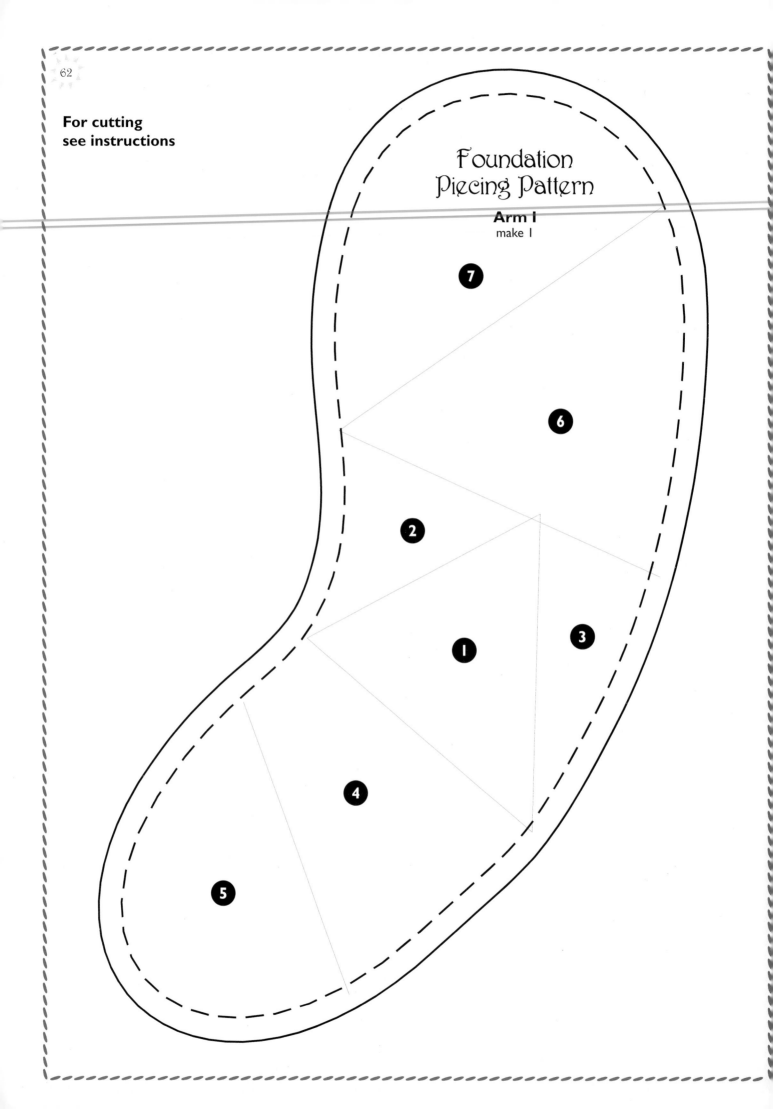

**For cutting
see instructions**

Foundation
Piecing Pattern

Arm I
make I

7

6

2

3

1

4

5

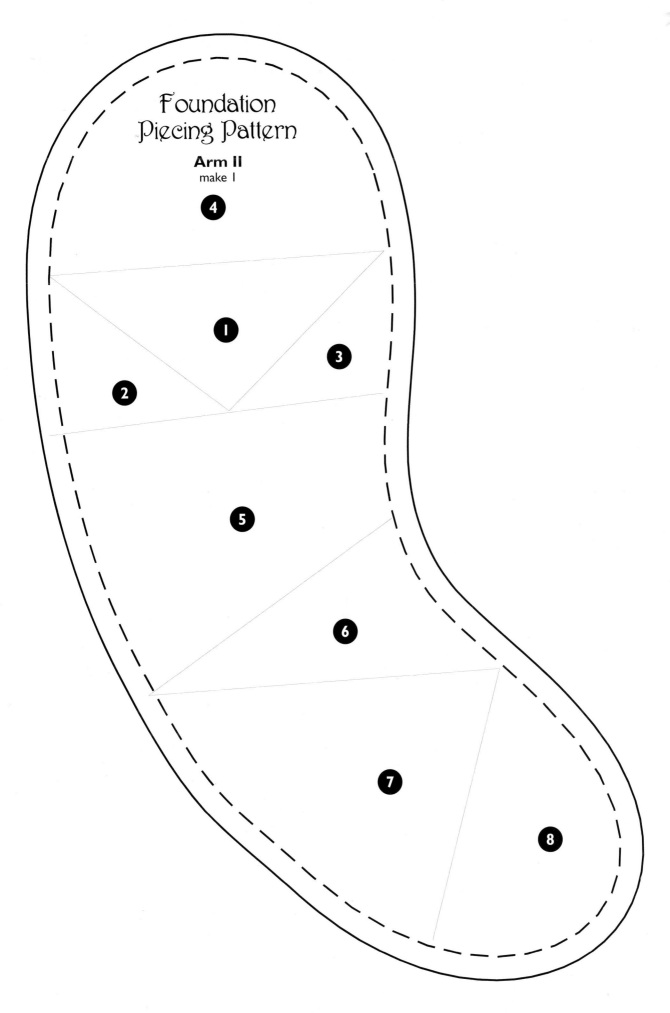

Foundation
Piecing Pattern

Arm II
make 1

64

**For cutting
see instructions**

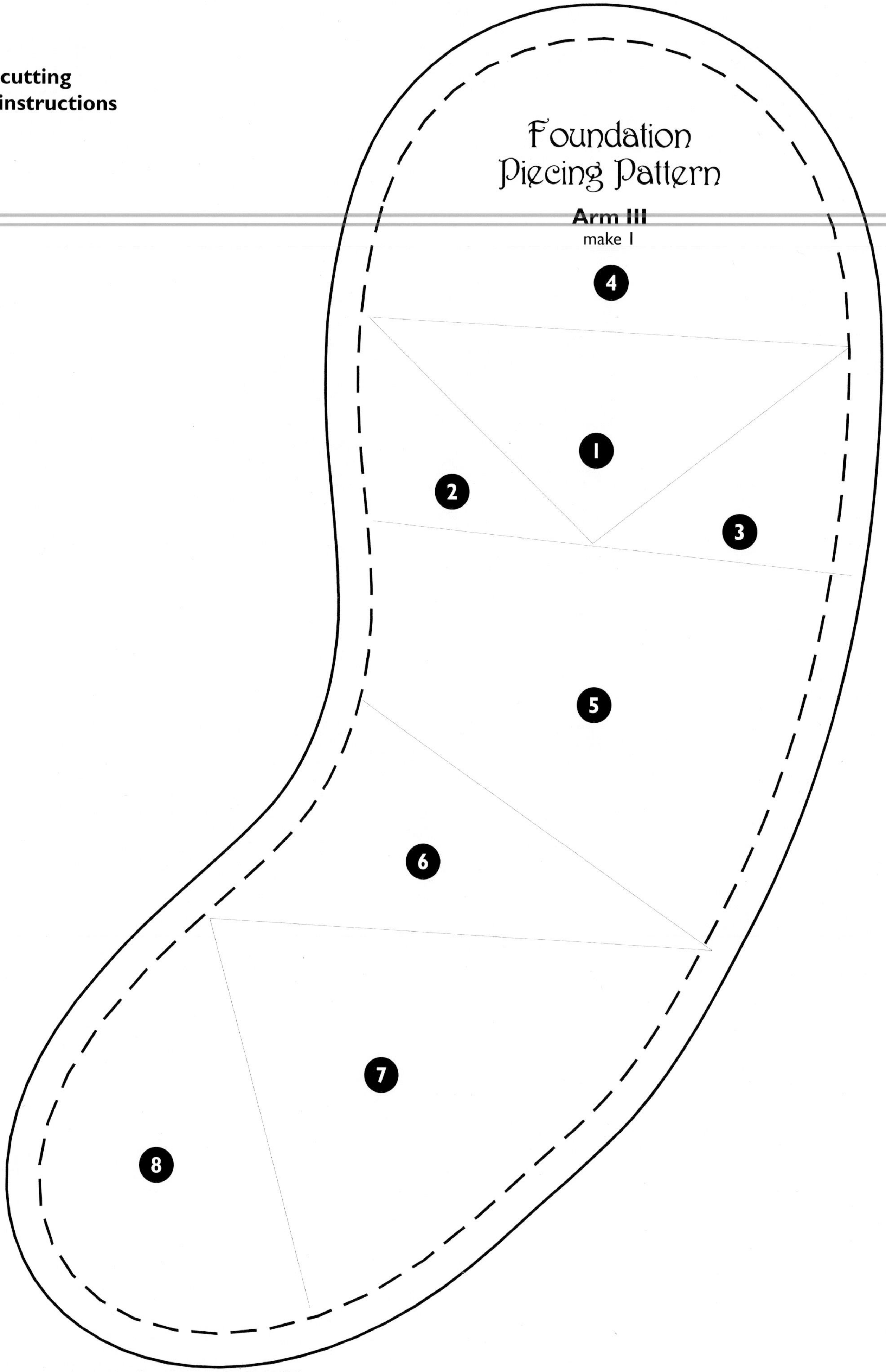

Foundation
Piecing Pattern

Arm III
make 1

④

①

②

③

⑤

⑥

⑦

⑧

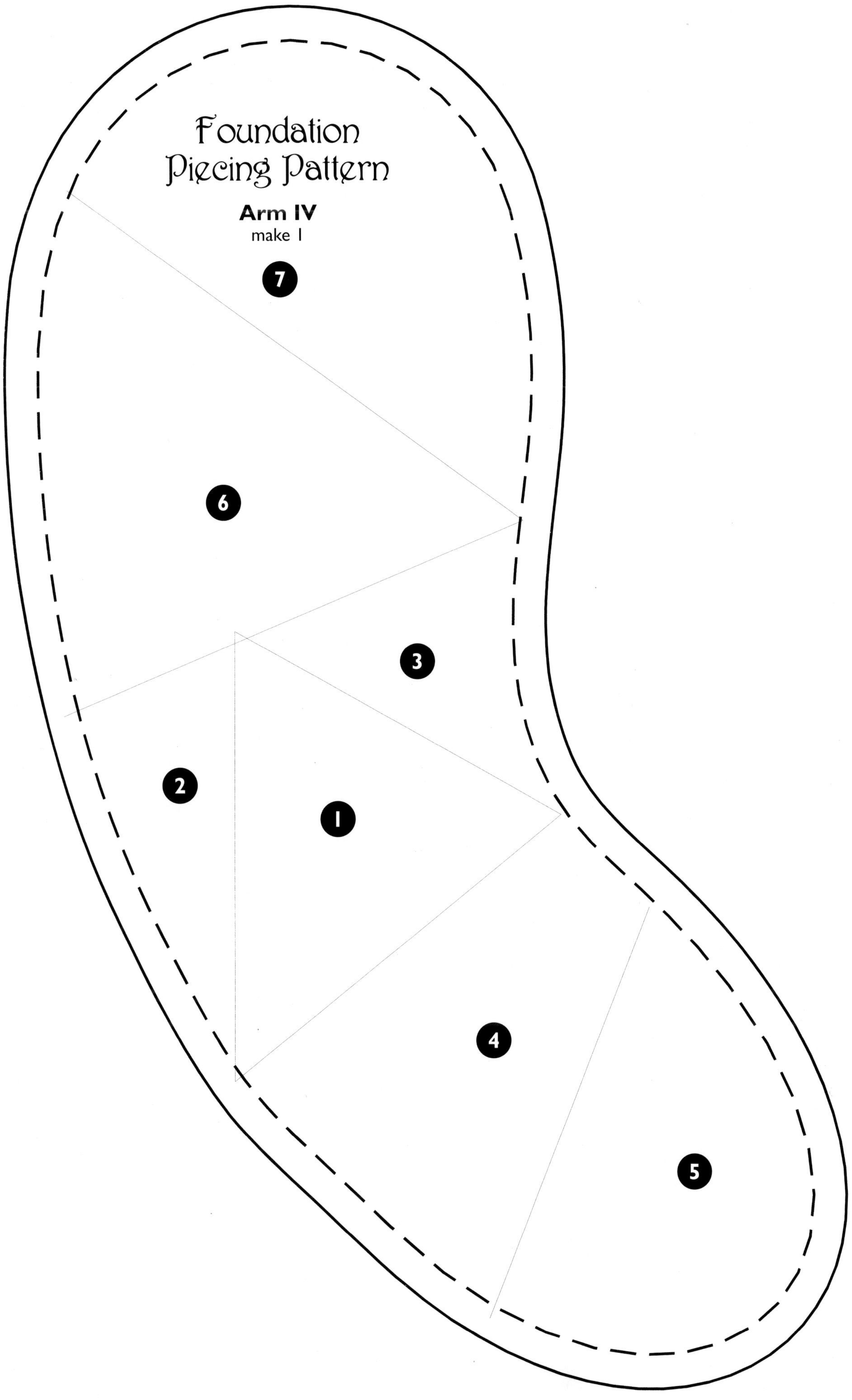

Foundation Piecing Pattern

Arm IV
make 1

7

6

3

2

1

4

5

66

Foundation Piecing Pattern

Body Front Left
make 1

top

tummy

side

For cutting see instructions

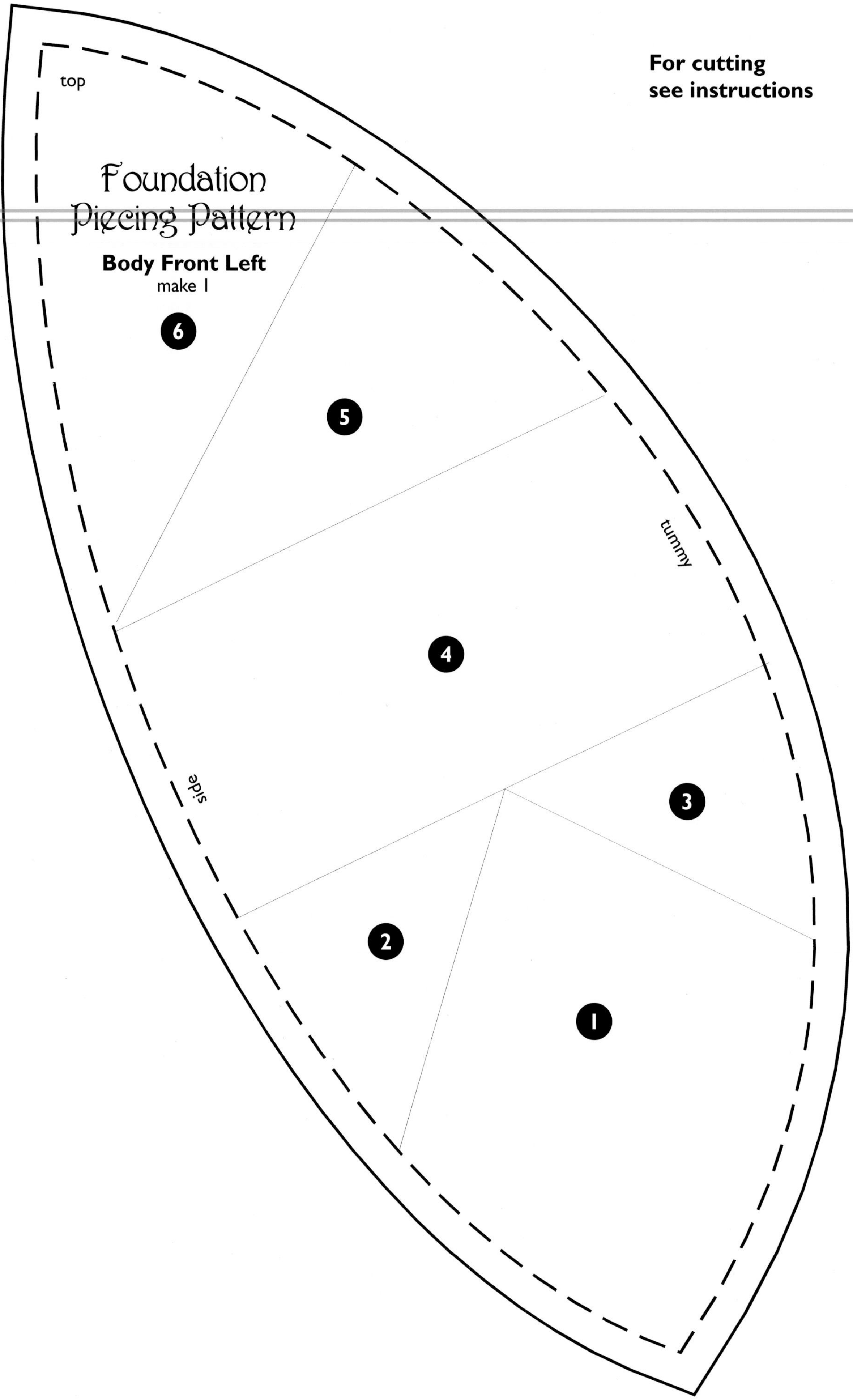

6

5

4

3

2

1

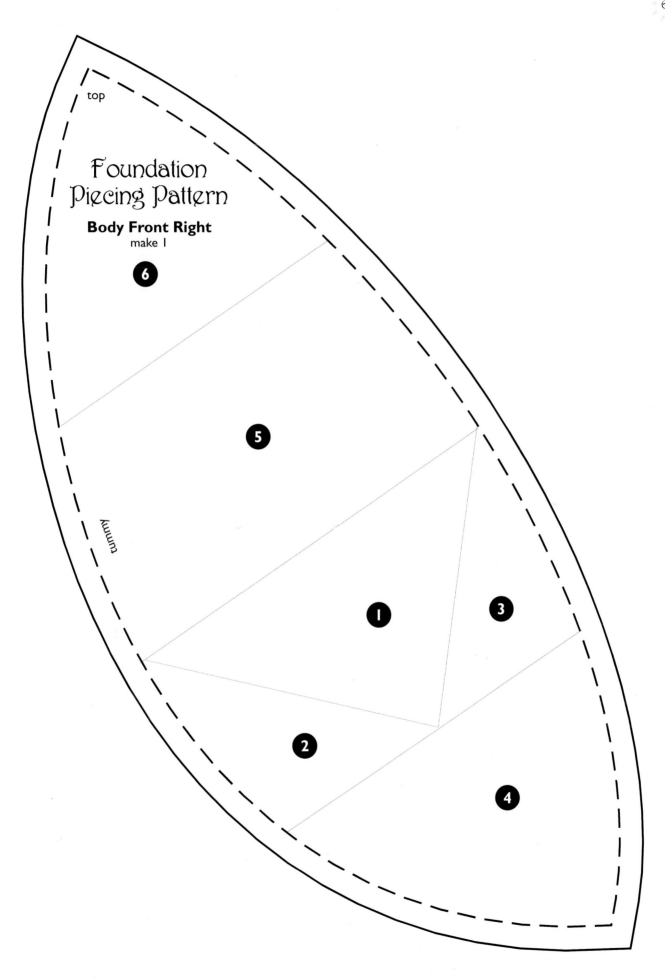

Foundation
Piecing Pattern

Body Front Right
make 1

top

tummy

6

5

1

3

2

4

top

Foundation
Piecing Pattern

Body Back Right

make 1

6

5

4

3

2

1

**For cutting
see instructions**

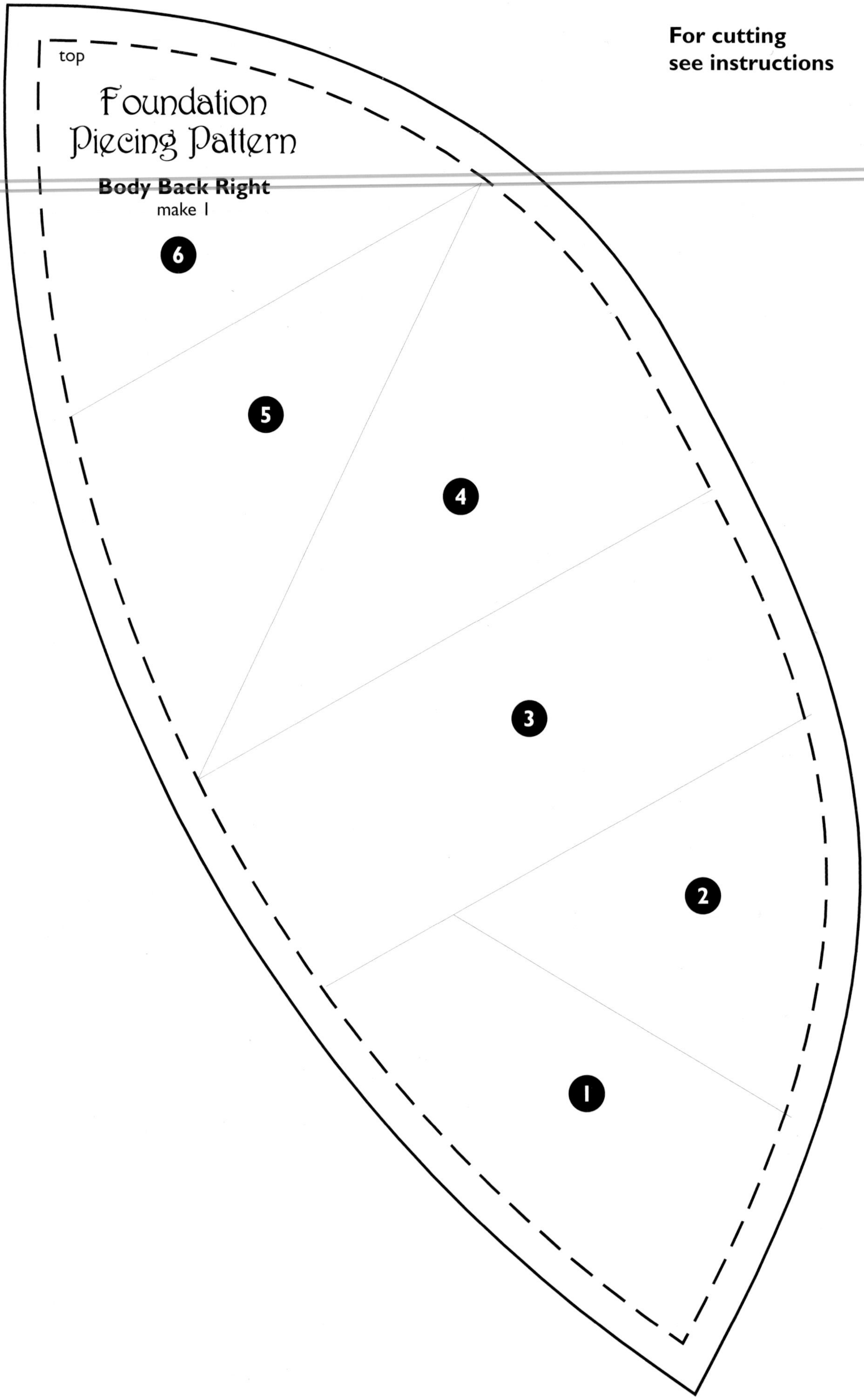

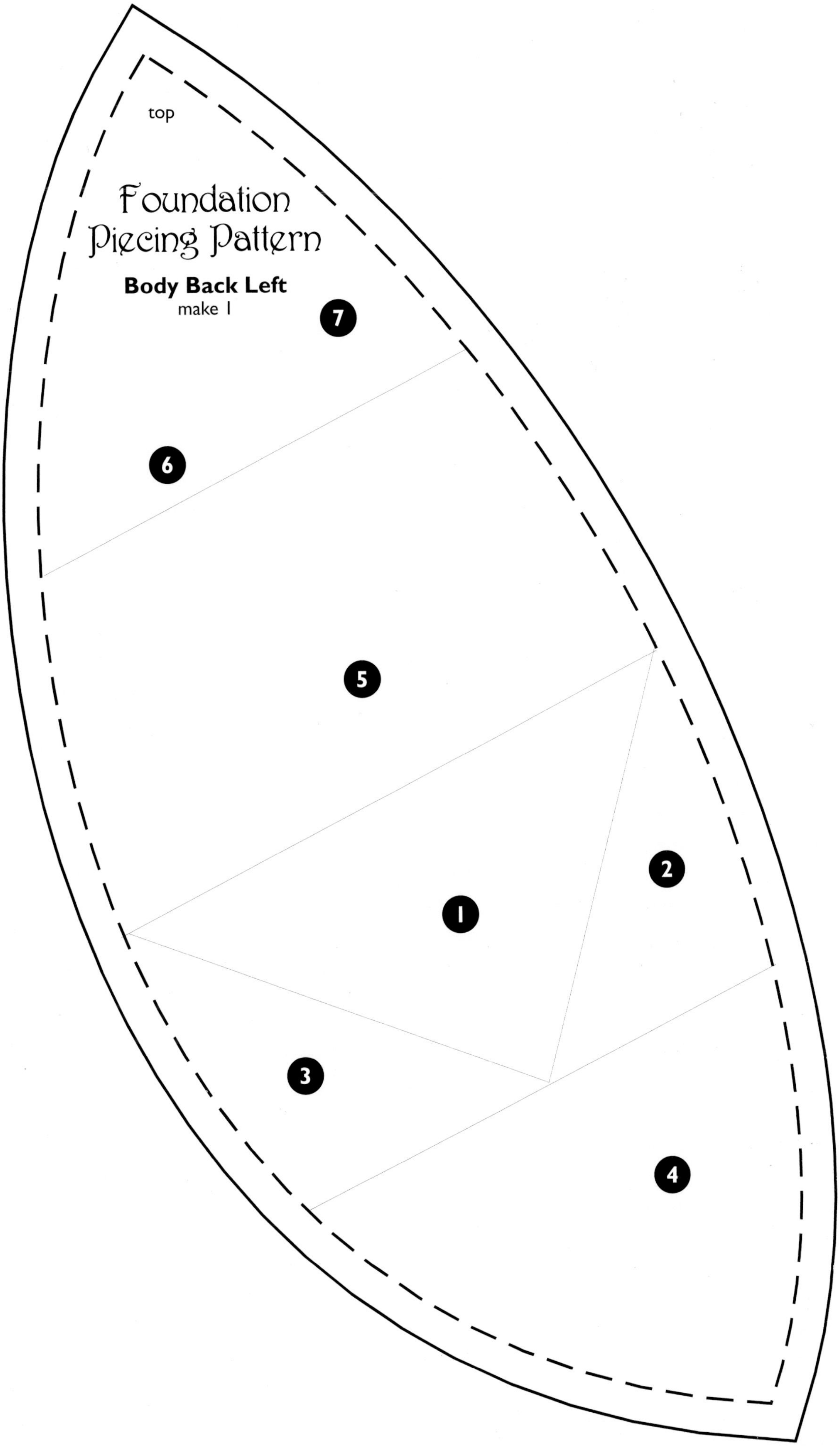

top

Foundation Piecing Pattern

Body Back Left
make 1

7

6

5

2

1

3

4

chapter five

Cubby Bear

Finished size: 18 inches (45.7cm)

A bit more contemporary in design, this bear features

large ears and a pouty snout. Two arm patterns, one

bent and one straighter, can be combined on one bear

for added posing possibilities; or choose one of the

arm patterns and stitch two of the same pose. ✿ Options include

appliquéd paw pads and long, fur eyelashes.

Highlighted sections treat face making in detail.

materials

* ⅓ yard (30.5cm) of fur fabric
* Matching thread
* Five sets of 2-inch (5cm) joints
* Two 14mm eyes
* Waxed dental floss or carpet thread
* Polyester fiberfill stuffing
* Perle cotton or embroidery floss
* Scrap of fabric for appliquéd paw pads (optional)
* Scrap of long pile black fur for eyelashes (optional)

instructions

Note: All seam allowances are ¼ inch (6mm).

1 Prepare the patterns and cut out the fur as instructed on pages 12 and 13.

2 With right sides together, pin the two body fronts along the center front seam. Stitch.

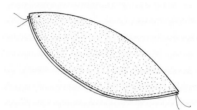

3 With right sides together, pin the two body backs along the center back seam. Stitch the seam from the top to the first dot, then from the second dot to the bottom. The opening left in the stitching between the two dots will provide access to the body for jointing and stuffing the bear.

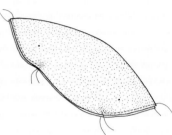

Appliquéd Paw Pads

For truly bearlike paws, machine appliqué fabric to the paws of your bear. Use any fabric desired for the appliqués: calico, suede, felt, corduroy, lamé—whatever suits your fancy and the character of the bear.

1. If the bear's fur is of long pile, begin by trimming the fur as instructed on page 86. Trim the paws as shown. Trim the entire foot pad.

2. Trace the paw pad markings onto the appliqué fabric. Pin in place on the foot or arm. Machine satin stitch around the appliqué, following the marked line. Trim close to the outside of the stitching. Satin stitch again over the previous stitching.

  Complete the bear.

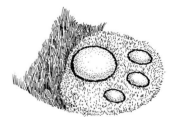

4 With right sides together, pin the body sides together, matching front left side to back left side and front right side to back right side. Stitch the sides from the dots down, leaving a small opening between the dots at the top to allow room for a neck joint. Turn the body right side out.

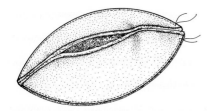

5 With right sides together, pin two arm pieces together. Stitch around the paw, leaving open between the dots at the top of the arm for turning and stuffing. Turn the arms right side out.

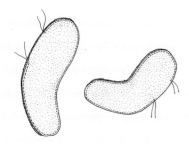

6 With right sides together, pin the legs together. Stitch from the dot at the front of the thigh down the leg and around the toes, ending at the foot. Stitch from the dot at the back of the thigh down to the back of the foot.

7 With right sides together, pin the foot pads to the bottom of the foot. Match the large dot on the paw pad to the front leg seam and the small dot to the back leg seam. Stitch, having the foot pad against the sewing machine bed. Turn the legs right side out.

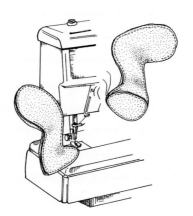

8 Pin the two side head pieces together, from the nose to the base of the neck. Stitch.

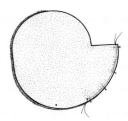

9 Pin the dot on the head gusset to the seam where the two head pieces meet at the tip of the nose. Match and pin the dot at the other neck edge of the gusset to the dot at the bottom of one head side. Pin the gusset to the nose and eye area. Ease the remainder of the

gusset to fit. Stitch. Repeat for the other side of the gusset. Turn head right side out.

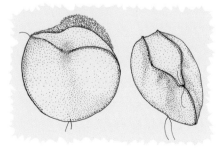

10 With right sides together, pin the two ears together. Stitch the rounded edges of the ears together, leaving the lower edge open. Turn.

Turn raw edge under ¹/₄ inch (6mm). Whipstitch closed. Repeat for the other ear.

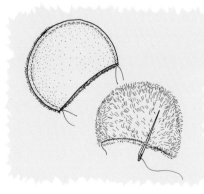

11 If using safety eyes, install them now, as instructed on page 46.

12 To stuff the head, begin with the nose, pushing table tennis ball–size pieces of fiberfill firmly into place with a stuffing tool. Continue with larger pieces of stuffing until the head is firmly stuffed to within about ³/₄ inch (1.8cm) of the neck opening. Check to be sure the stuffing is even, restuffing if need be.

13 Joint the bear as instructed on page 44.

14 If using glass eyes, install them as instructed on page 46.

⑮ Stuff the body, arms and legs. Stitch the openings closed using a ladderstitch as instructed on page 17.

⑯ Decide where you want the ears. Pin them in place. Stitch them to the head in a circular motion, sewing through the ear at the top of the circle and the head on the bottom of the circle.

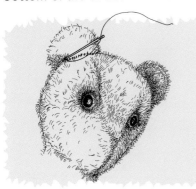

Eyelashes

Add a bit of whimsy to your bear by giving it long, flirty lashes. It takes no time at all!

Before installing the eye:
1. Cut a piece of black or brown long pile fur about ¹/₄ inch (6mm) or so larger than the eye.

2. Using an awl, make a hole in the center of the fur. From the right side of the fur, push the shaft of the eye into the hole.

3. Install the eye as instructed on page 46.

4. Trim the eyelash fur backing as close to the eye as possible. Trim the fur pile from the bottom and sides of the eye. Using a pin, pull the fur at the top and sides from under the eye. Trim fur as desired.

Making Faces: Embroidery

I use two methods for embroidering the nose: one uses vertical stitches, the other horizontal stitches. I find the former easier for beginners, especially when paired with a felt template.

Successful nose embroidery requires practice. Students often "unembroider" twice before achieving a satisfactory nose. Experiment to find the method that works best for you.

1. Clip the fur where the nose is to go so that stray hairs won't poke through your nose stitching. Following the nose pattern, cut a piece of felt the same color as your embroidery floss. Glue the felt in place. Thread a tapestry needle with a length of embroidery thread or perle cotton. Knot one end.

2. Push the needle into the fabric under the felt nose and come out at the center top of the nose, just above the felt. Push the needle back into the fabric at the center bottom of the nose just below the felt and out at the top of the nose, just to the left of where the thread first emerged.

3. Push the needle in at the bottom of the nose, to the left of the thread, and out at the top, just to the right of the thread.

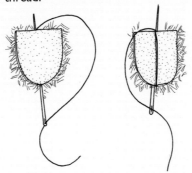

4. Continue working stitches across the nose area in this manner, making a stitch on one side of the nose and then the other, checking to be sure the nose is turning out evenly, until the felt is covered.

5. After the last stitch, come up at the center bottom of the nose. Push the needle into the fabric at the left hand corner of the mouth, about ⁵/₈ inch

(1.5cm) below the nose and ⁵/₈ inch to the left of the seam. Bring the needle out of the fabric on the seamline and about ⁵/₈ inch below the nose so that it runs between the thread and the left corner of the mouth. (Note: measurements are for an 18-inch [45.7cm] bear; adjust the length of your stitches to suit your bear.) Push the needle back into the fabric at the right side of the mouth and out through the center of the nose.

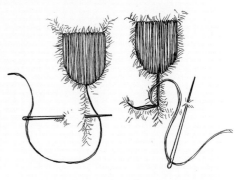

If you are unhappy with your bear's smile you may change it at this point by removing the thread from the needle and pulling the mouth stitches out. Rethread the needle and try again. When you are satisfied with the bear's mouth, fasten the thread using the lost thread method on page 13.

Thread tension is one key to a great teddy bear nose. When you pull the thread after each stitch, pull it just until it rests gently on the fur beneath. This way the stitches will have the same tension and lie at the same level.
   Kathy Semone, Rockville, Maryland

If you've made a number of stitches and then discover that one stitch several stitches back was too tight or too loose, resist the temptation to try to even them out. Remove the stitches instead, as trying to adjust them always makes a mess.

Making Faces: Positioning for Expression

Your teddy bear can wear many expressions. From sweet and winsome to heart-wrenchingly sad, a simple change in the placement of the eyes, the angle of the mouth embroidery, or the position of the ears can change the bear's personality.

To experiment with the possibilities, cut a nose from black felt and use dark, large head pins to simulate eyes. Move these around on the bear's head until the expression pleases you.

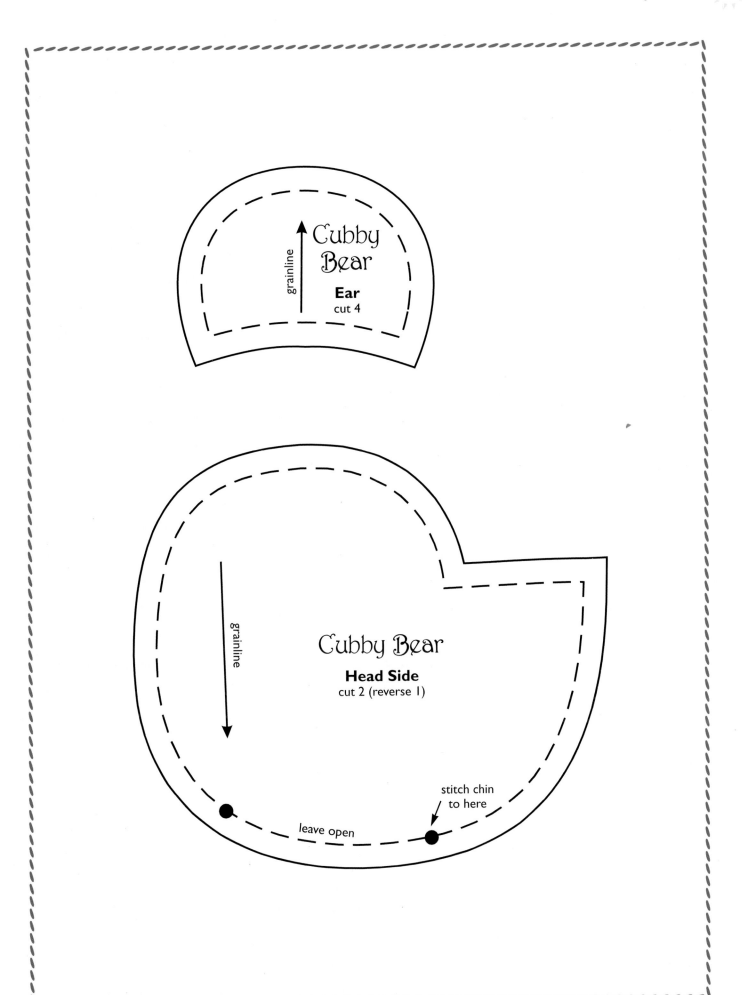

Cubby
Bear

grainline

Ear
cut 4

Cubby Bear

Head Side
cut 2 (reverse 1)

grainline

stitch chin
to here

leave open

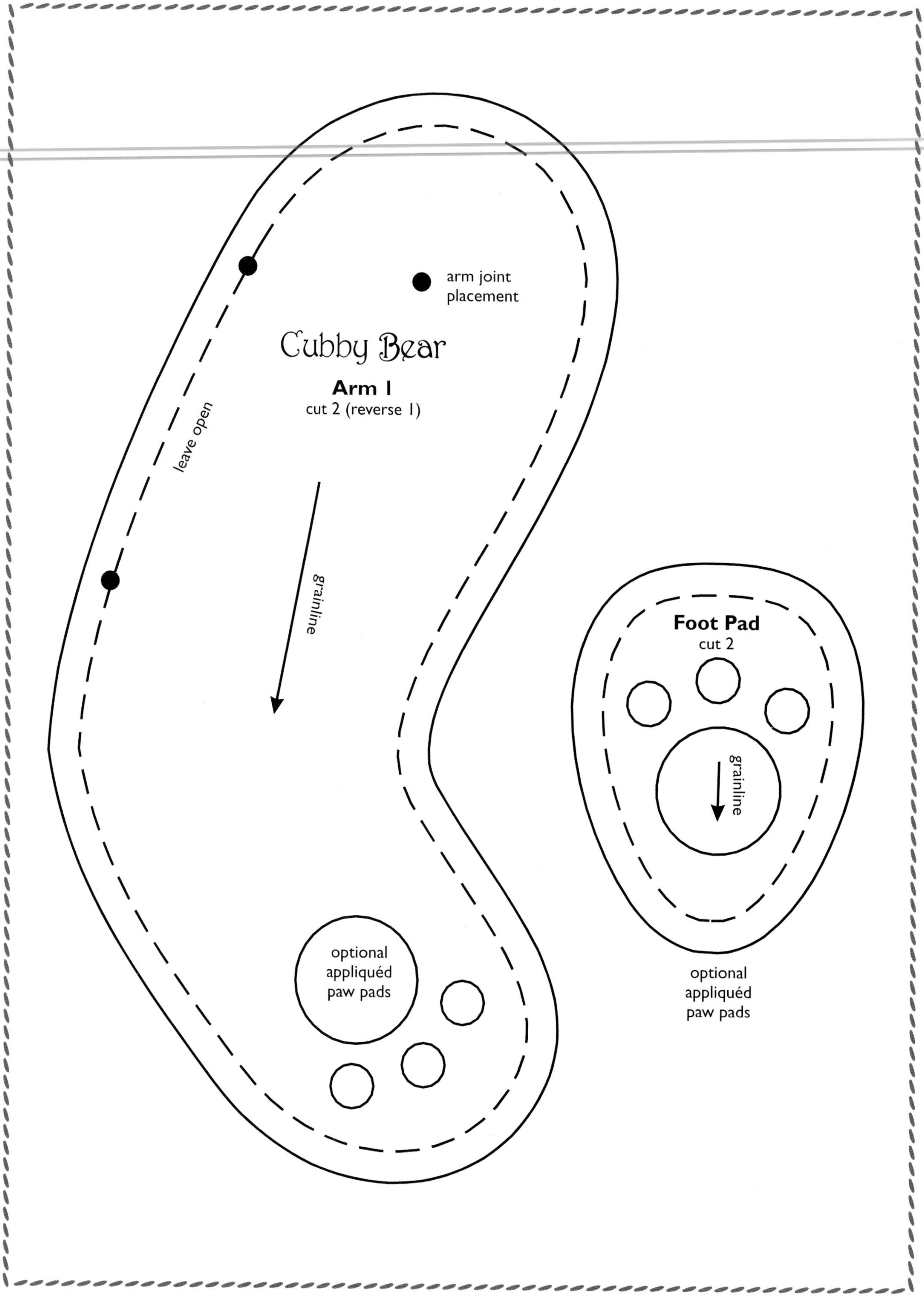

Cubby Bear

Arm 1
cut 2 (reverse 1)

arm joint
placement

leave open

grainline

optional
appliquéd
paw pads

Foot Pad
cut 2

grainline

optional
appliquéd
paw pads

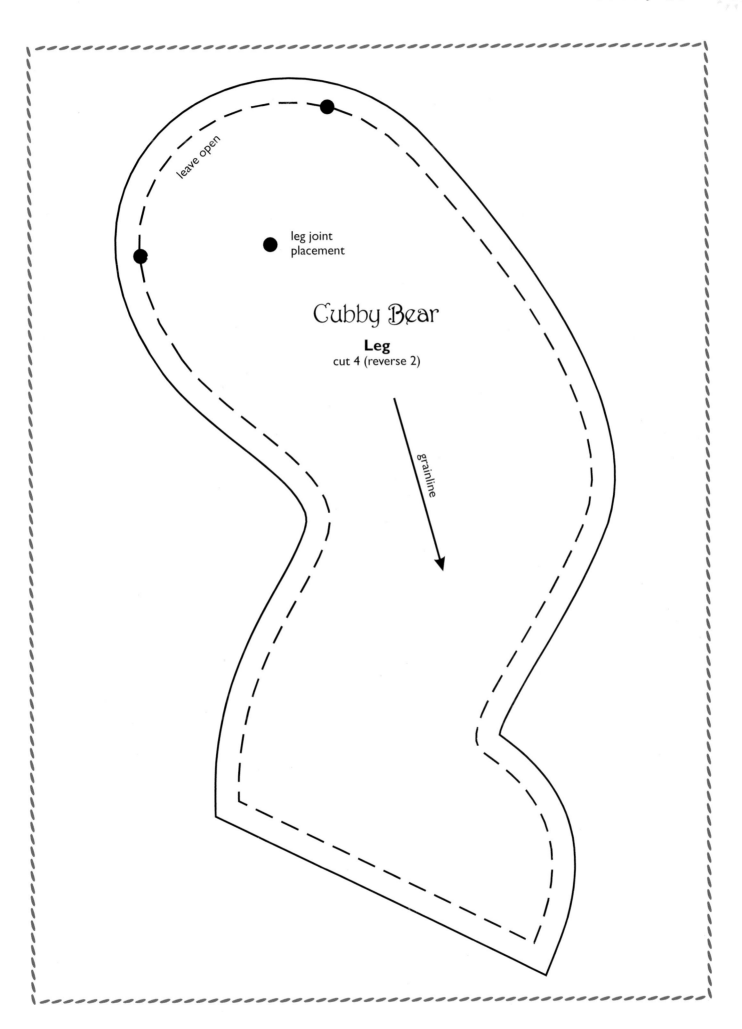

leave open

leg joint
placement

Cubby Bear

Leg
cut 4 (reverse 2)

grainline

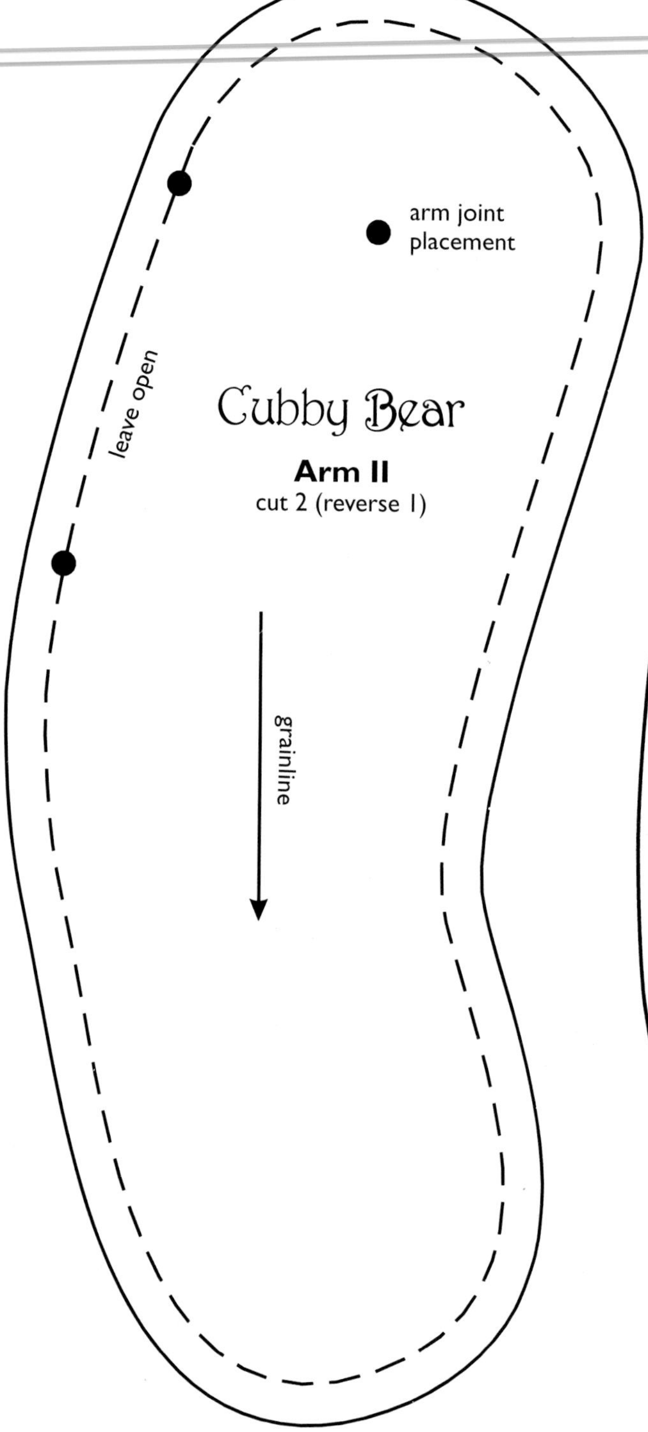

arm joint
placement

leave open

Cubby Bear

Arm II
cut 2 (reverse 1)

grainline

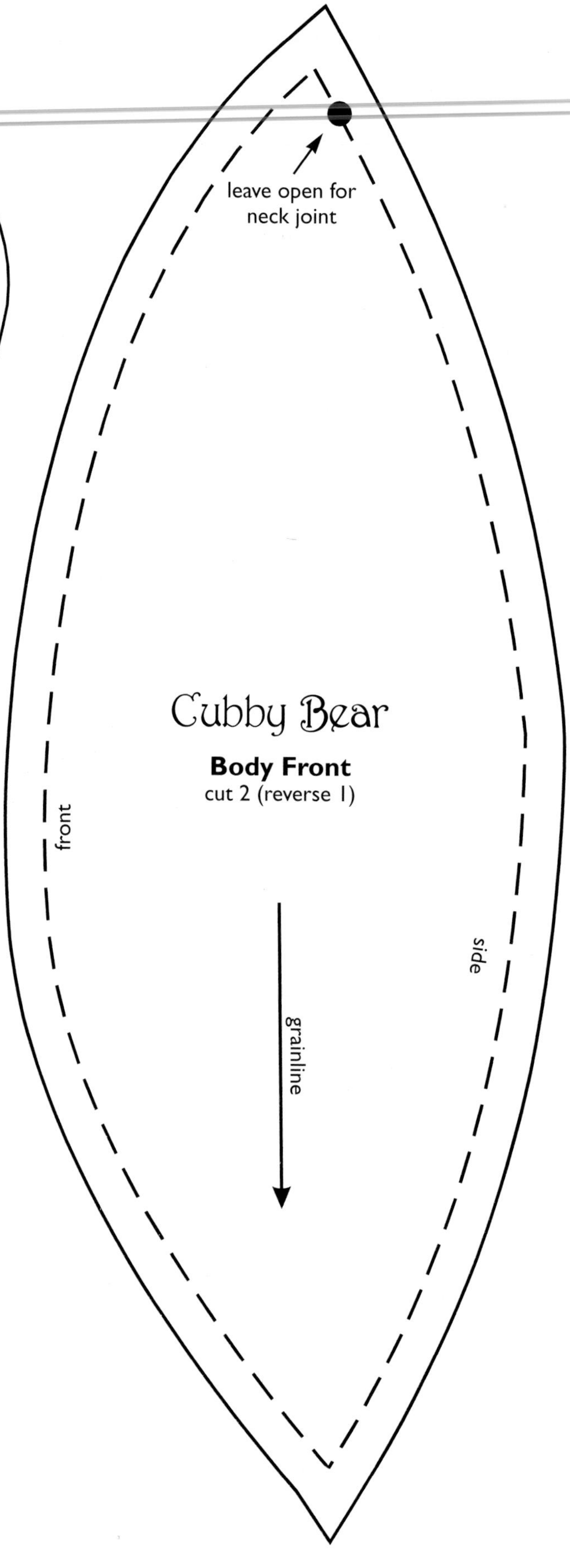

leave open for
neck joint

Cubby Bear

Body Front
cut 2 (reverse 1)

front

side

grainline

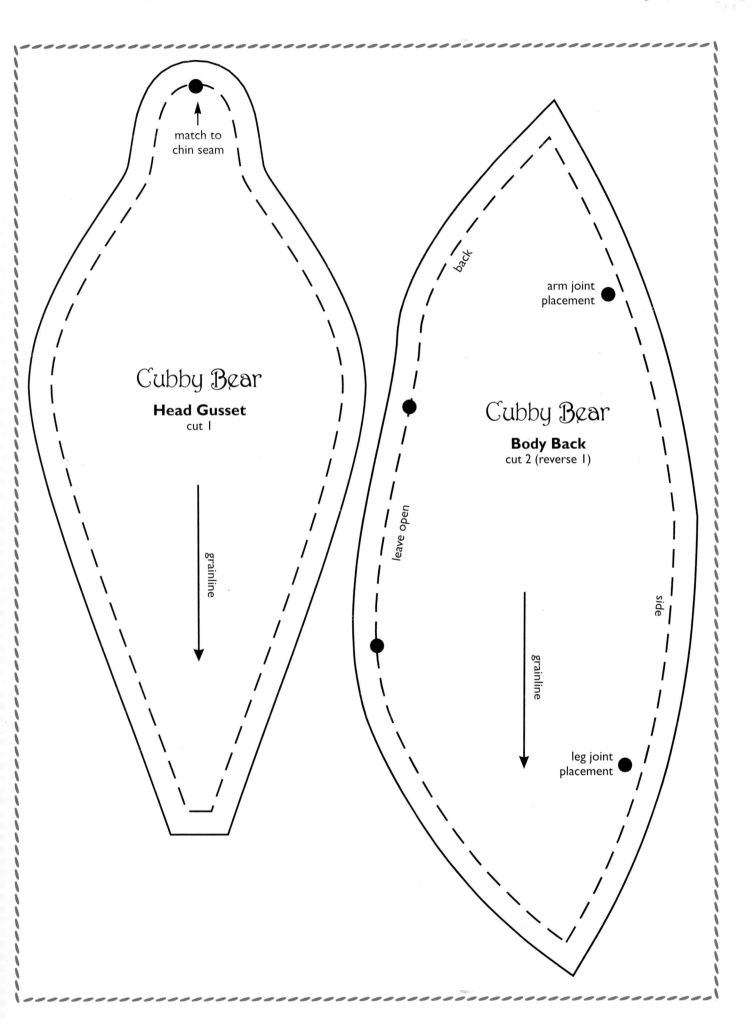

match to
chin seam

Cubby Bear

Head Gusset
cut 1

grainline

back

arm joint
placement

Cubby Bear

Body Back
cut 2 (reverse 1)

leave open

side

grainline

leg joint
placement

chapter six

Fashion Bear with Ballerina Variation

Finished size: 14 inches (35.5cm) or 23 inches (58.4cm)

Dress this bear in a fashionable outfit, turn her into a bride or a

ballerina, or leave her —as many prefer—

just a plain bear. I've included the bear

pattern in a smaller size, standing 14 inches (35.5cm) tall, as well

as the 23-inch (58.4cm) size, and patterns for short and

long legs and small and large ears.

materials

* ⁵/₈ yard (57cm) of synthetic fur fabric (¹/₄ yard [22.8cm] for 14-inch [35.5cm] bear)
* Matching thread
* Small piece of suede or wool felt for paw pads and soles
* Five sets of 2¹/₂-inch (6.3cm) joints (1³/₄-inch [4.4cm] for 14-inch [35.5cm] bear)
* Two 18mm eyes (10mm for 14-inch [35.5cm] bear)
* Waxed dental floss or carpet thread
* Polyester fiberfill stuffing
* Perle cotton or embroidery floss

instructions

Note: All seam allowances are ¹/₄ inch (6mm).

1 Prepare the patterns and cut out the fur as instructed on pages 12 and 13.

2 Pin the two body backs together along the center back seam. Stitch the seam from the top to the first dot. Stitch from the second dot to the bottom. The opening left in the stitching between the two dots will provide access to the body for jointing and stuffing the bear.

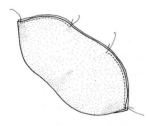

3 Pin the body backs to the body front. Stitch, leaving an opening between the dots for jointing.

4 Pin paw pads to inner arms, right sides together. Stitch.

5 Right sides together, pin the outer arms to the inner arms, with the paw pads opened. Stitch around the paw, leaving an opening between the dots at the back of the arm for turning and stuffing. Turn the arms right side out.

6 With right sides together, pin two leg pieces together. Stitch from the dot at the top back of the thigh over the top of the leg, down the front of the leg and around the toes, ending at the foot. Stitch from the dot at the back of the thigh down to the back of the foot.

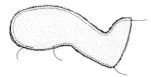

7 Pin the foot pads to the bottom of the feet, right sides together. Match the large dot on the paw pad to the front leg seam and the small dot to the back leg seam. Stitch, with the paw pad against the sewing machine bed. Turn the legs right side out.

8 Pin the two side head pieces together, from the nose to the base of the neck. Stitch.

9 Pin the dot on the gusset to the seam where the two head pieces meet at the tip of the nose. Pin one side of the gusset from the tip of the nose to the base of the neck, easing the gusset to fit as you go. Stitch. Repeat for the other side. Turn right side out.

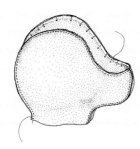

10 Pin and sew the rounded edge of the ears, right sides together, leaving the lower edge open. Turn. Turn under 1/4 inch (6mm) along raw edges. Whipstitch closed.

11 If using safety eyes, install them now as instructed on page 46.

12 To stuff the head, begin with the nose, pushing table tennis ball–size pieces of fiberfill firmly into place with a stuffing tool. Continue with larger pieces of stuffing until the head is firmly stuffed to within about 3/4 inch (1.8cm) of the neck opening. Check to be sure the stuffing is even, restuffing if necessary.

13 If using glass eyes, install them now as instructed on page 46.

14 Joint the bear as instructed on page 44.

15 Stuff the body, arms, and legs. With a ladderstitch (see page 17), stitch the openings closed.

16 Decide where you want the ears and pin them in place. Stitch the ears to the head in a circular motion, sewing through the ear at the top of the circle and the head on the bottom of the circle.

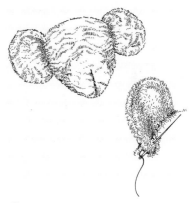

17 Turn to page 75 for instructions to embroider the nose and mouth.

Finishing Touches

Embroidering Claws

Embroidered claws add a realistic touch to a teddy bear.

1. Referring to the illustration, place pins in the bear's paws to mark the position of stitches.

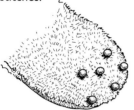

2. Thread a long needle with embroidery floss or perle cotton. Insert the needle in the paw. Come out at the end of the paw, and go back into the hole the needle just emerged from. Repeat, this time emerging at pin 1. Remove the pins as you come to them.

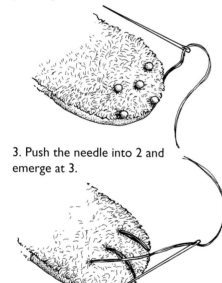

3. Push the needle into 2 and emerge at 3.

4. Go back in at 4 and out at 5.

5. Push the needle in at 6 and emerge anywhere in the paw area. Go back into the same hole the needle just emerged from. Repeat. Come out in the paw. Clip the thread close to the fur.

Trimming Fur Pile

Fur pile is often shortened on bears' noses and paw and foot pads. For fabrics with a different color underfur or for tipped fabrics, trimming the pile exposes the second color.

Some bear makers find it easier to trim pile after cutting the pieces, but before construction. Others shorten pile after assembling the bear. Either way, hold the scissors parallel to the fur's backing and aim for a smooth level surface. Practice on fur scraps first.

Ears

For a smooth seam along the top curve of a bear's ears, trim the fur from the seam allowances before stitching the ear pieces together. This makes the seam much less noticeable.

To do so, lay the ear on a table. Hold the scissors nearly flat against the tabletop and snip carefully, trimming the pile even with the backing.

To give the ears a realistic cupped look, try these two techniques.

Cut the curved edge of the front ear piece a little smaller—about 1/8 inch (3mm) for a medium-size bear—than the back of the ear. When you sew the ears together, the front ear piece will pull the back piece toward the front. This is especially nice where two different fabrics are used, as with a lighter color for the front (inner) ear.

After turning the seam allowances to the inside, gather the front (inner) ear along the lower edge. Pull up on the gathering as desired. Whipstitch to secure. This will produce a nice puckered ear.

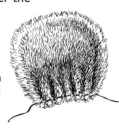

Shaving noses bothered me until I bought an electric moustache shaver. It is battery operated and works like a charm!

Warner Lord
Madison, Connecticut

clothing
Bride's outfit

materials

- ²/₃ yard (61cm) of fabric
- Matching thread
- 18-inch (45.7cm) -long piece of ¹/₄-inch (6mm) -wide elastic
- Appliqué for front of dress, approximately 5 inches (12.7cm) square
- Twelve ¹/₂-inch (1.2cm) buttons
- 2 yards (1.8cm) of 1-inch (2.5cm) -wide ribbon for slipper ties and sleeve bows
- Wired flowers for headpiece (found in bridal department of fabric stores)
- 1 yard (91.5cm) of lace with one embroidered edge
- Flowers and ribbon for bouquet

instructions

Note: All seam allowances are ¹/₄ inch (6mm).

1 Prepare the patterns and cut out the fabric pieces. Cut the skirt 12 × 32 inches (30.5 × 81.3cm). For the skirt overlay, cut the embroidered edge of the lace 11¹/₂ inches (29.2cm) wide. Reserve the remaining piece of lace for the veil.

2 Stitch two bodice back pieces to a bodice front piece at shoulders and side seams. Repeat for the second set to make lining.

3 Right sides together, pin the bodice lining to the bodice front. Stitch along the neck and center back openings. Turn right side out. Press.

4 Press 1¹/₂ inches (3.8cm) to the wrong side along the sleeve hem edge. Cut the elastic in half. Stitch one piece of elastic over the pressed edge of the sleeve, stretching the elastic as you stitch. Repeat for the second sleeve.

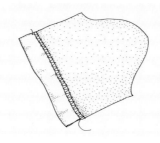

5 Stitch the underarm sleeve seams.

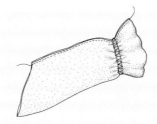

6 Gather the top, curved edge of each sleeve, between the dots. Right sides together, pin the sleeve to the bodice armhole, treating the bodice and lining as one layer. Pull up on the gathering to fit. Stitch. Repeat for the second sleeve.

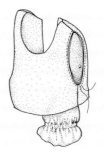

7 Press ¹/₄ inch (6mm) to the inside twice along one long edge of the skirt. Topstitch.

8 Right sides together, stitch the center back of the skirt using a ¹/₂-inch (1.2cm) seam, starting 2 inches (5cm) below the top.

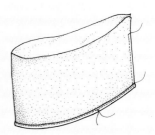

Press the seam open. Turn the raw edges of the seam allowances ¹/₄ inch (6mm) to the wrong side. Topstitch. Turn the skirt right side out.

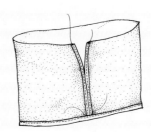

9 Right sides together, stitch the 12-inch (30.5cm) -long edges of the lace overlay together. Put the skirt inside the lace, with the wrong side of the lace against the right side of the skirt. Gather the top edge of the skirt and lace as one.

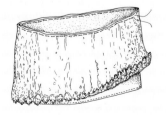

10 Right sides together, pin the skirt to the bodice, leaving the bodice lining free. Adjust the gathering to fit. Stitch.

11 Turn the lining 1/4 inch (6mm) to the inside. Slipstitch.

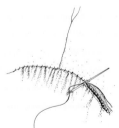

12 Hand sew the appliqué to the front of the dress.

13 Put the dress on the bear. Cut the ribbon into six pieces. Reserve four pieces for the slipper ties. Make bows with the two remaining pieces and tack to the sleeves.

Slippers

1 Right sides together, pin and stitch two slipper pieces along front and back seams. Repeat for the two lining pieces.

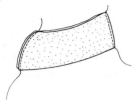

2 Right sides together, pin a slipper bottom to a slipper. Stitch. Repeat for the lining pieces, leaving a 1/2-inch (1.2cm) opening for turning.

3 Turn one slipper right side out. Pin the end of one piece of ribbon to the dot on the slipper as shown. Repeat with the remaining ribbon.

With right sides together, put one slipper inside the other, matching the top raw edges. Stitch, making certain not to catch the ribbon in the stitching.

4 Turn right side out through the opening. Slipstitch opening closed. Piece with the opening should be inside the slipper, making it the lining. Repeat for the second slipper.

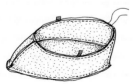

5 Put the slippers on the bear and tie the ribbons into bows.

Headpiece

1 Bend the wire ends of the headpiece back and loop them together to form a circle. Place on the bear's head. Trim if necessary.

2 Finish the edges of the lace remaining from the skirt with a narrow zigzag stitch. Gather 12 inches (30.5cm) from one edge.

3 Pull up on the gathering. Place the veil at the back of the head, having the gathering under the wired flowers, as shown below.

Ballerina

materials

* ³/₈ **yard (34.2cm) of satin fabric**
* **Matching thread**
* ¹/₃ **yard (30.5cm) of tulle**
* **14-inch (35.5cm) -long piece of ¹/₄-inch (6mm) -wide elastic**
* **2¹/₂ yards (2.2m) of ³/₈-inch (1cm) -wide ribbon for dress back ties**
* **1 yard (91.5cm) of 1-inch (2.5cm) -wide ribbon**
* **2 yards (1.8m) of ³/₈-inch (1cm) -wide ribbon for slippers**

instructions

Note: All seam allowances are ¹/₄ inch (6mm) unless otherwise noted.

❶ Prepare patterns and fabric as instructed on pages 12 and 13.

❷ Right sides together, stitch the two bodysuit back pieces along the center back seam from the dot down. Repeat for the two remaining pieces, which will be the lining.

❸ With right sides together, stitch one front to one of the back sets along side edges. Repeat with the lining pieces.

❹ Cut the narrower ribbon into ten pieces, each 9 inches (22.8cm) long. Set four pieces aside for shoulder ties. Pin each of the remaining pieces to a dot along the back opening of the bodysuit, on the right side of the fabric. Baste.

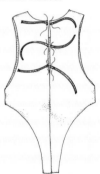

❺ Right sides together, stitch the bodysuit to the lining along armholes and neck edge. At each side of the bodysuit back, pivot at the top of the neck edge and continue down to the dot where you started stitching the center back seam, catching the ribbon in the seam. Turn right side out. Press.

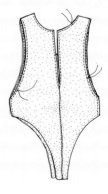

6 Fold the raw edges at the front shoulder seams ¹/₄ inch (6mm) to the wrong side. Press. Insert a piece of ribbon into the bodysuit at each shoulder seam. Topstitch. Repeat for the remaining shoulders.

7 Right sides together, stitch the crotch seam of the bodysuit. Repeat for the lining.

8 Press ¹/₄ inch (6mm) to the wrong side along each leg opening of both the bodysuit and the lining. Topstitch together.

Tutu

1 Cut the tulle into two pieces, each 12 × 22 inches (30.5 × 55.8cm).

2 Seam the short edges of one piece, using a narrow zigzag stitch. Repeat for the second piece.

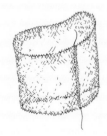

3 Put one tulle piece inside the other matching seams. Fold top raw edge down to meet other raw edge. Topstitch ³/₈ inch (1cm) from the folded edge, leaving a ¹/₂-inch (1.2cm) opening in the stitching.

4 Attach a safety pin to one end of the elastic. Insert elastic through the opening, along the casing, emerging from the opening. Overlap the elastic ends and stitch.

Slippers

Follow the instructions for the slippers on page 89 for the Bride Bear. Tie the ribbons as shown in the photograph below.

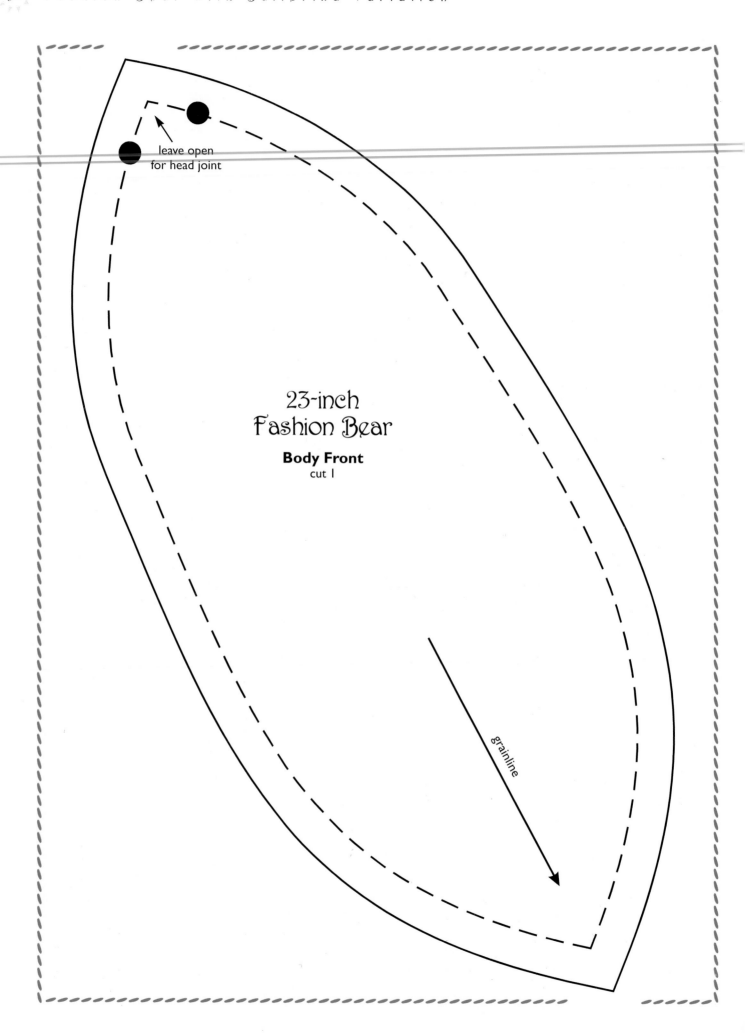

leave open
for head joint

23-inch
Fashion Bear

Body Front
cut 1

grainline

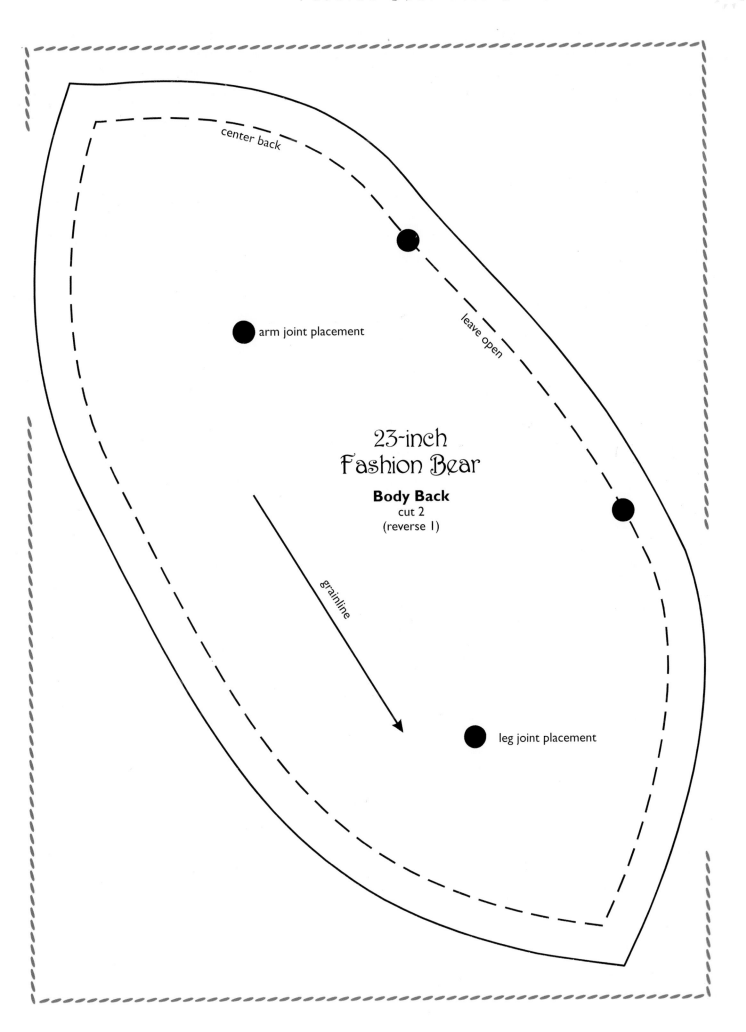

center back

leave open

arm joint placement

23-inch
Fashion Bear

Body Back
cut 2
(reverse 1)

grainline

leg joint placement

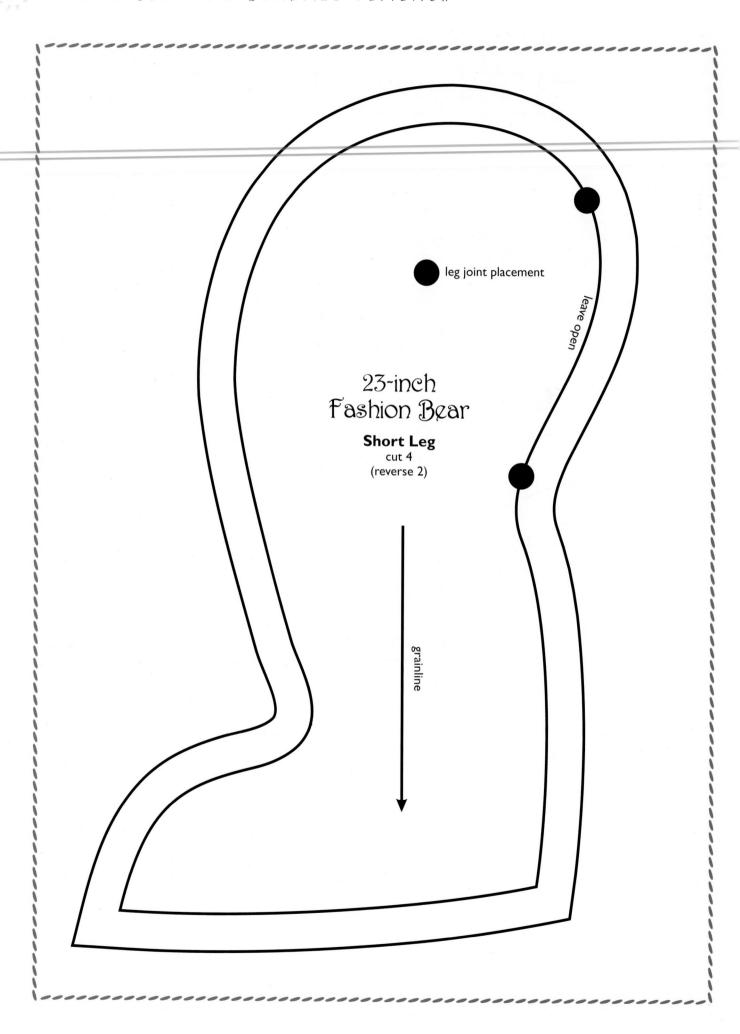

leg joint placement

leave open

23-inch
Fashion Bear

Short Leg
cut 4
(reverse 2)

grainline

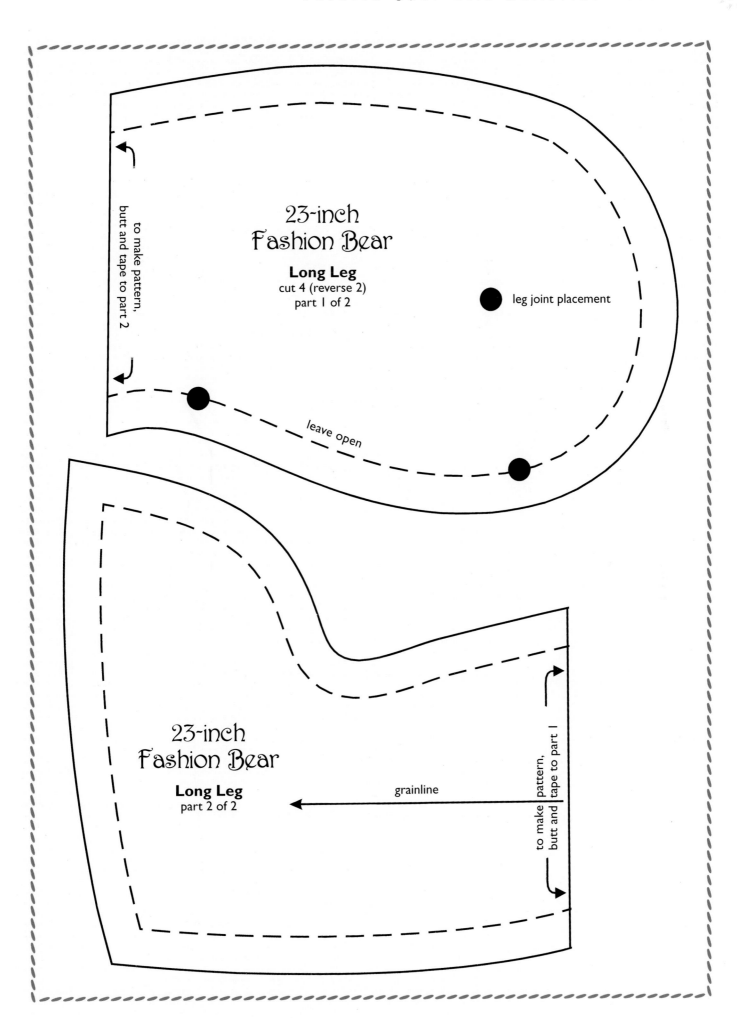

23-inch
Fashion Bear

Long Leg
cut 4 (reverse 2)
part 1 of 2

leg joint placement

to make pattern,
butt and tape to part 2

leave open

23-inch
Fashion Bear

Long Leg
part 2 of 2

grainline

to make pattern,
butt and tape to part 1

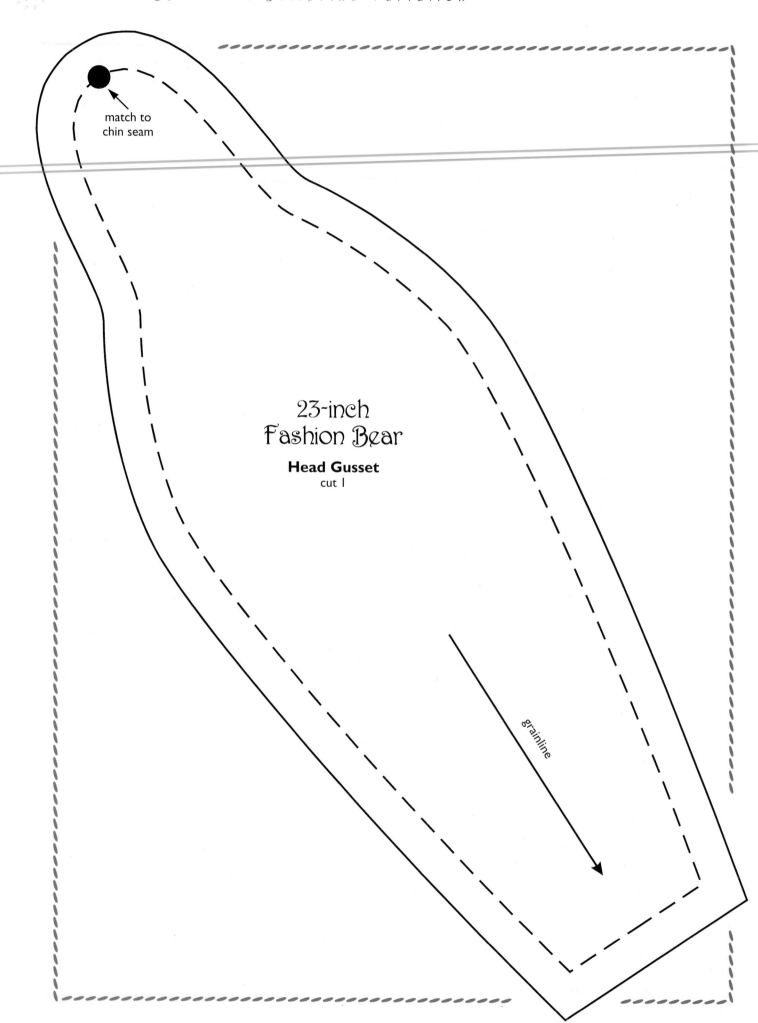

match to
chin seam

23-inch
Fashion Bear

Head Gusset
cut 1

grainline

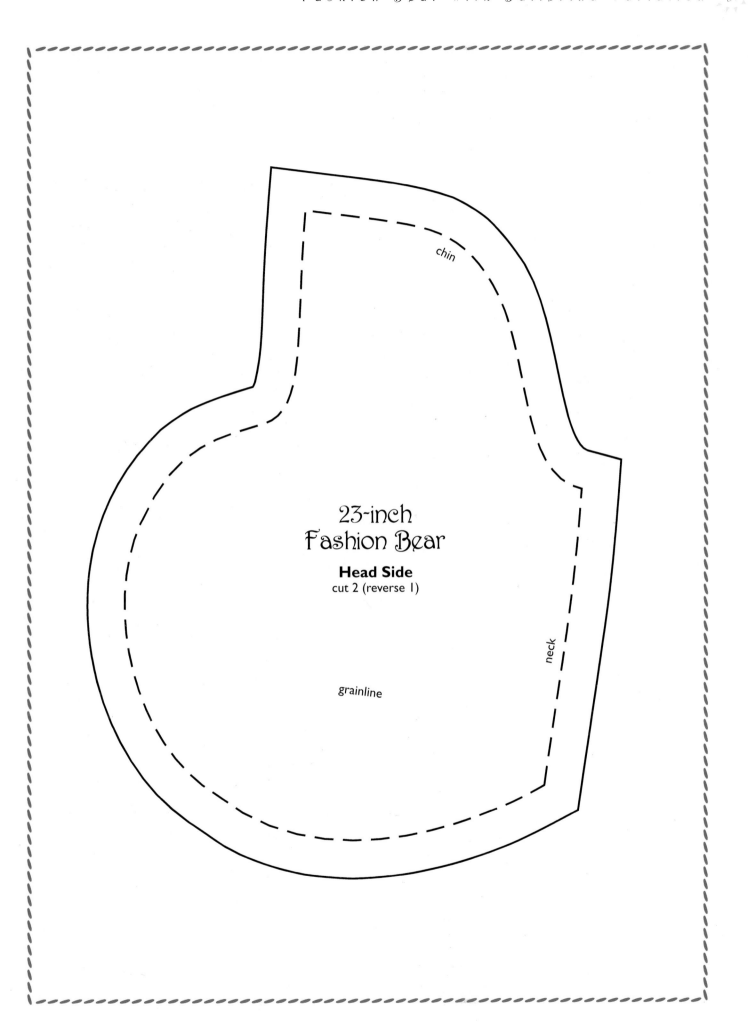

23-inch
Fashion Bear

Head Side
cut 2 (reverse 1)

chin

neck

grainline

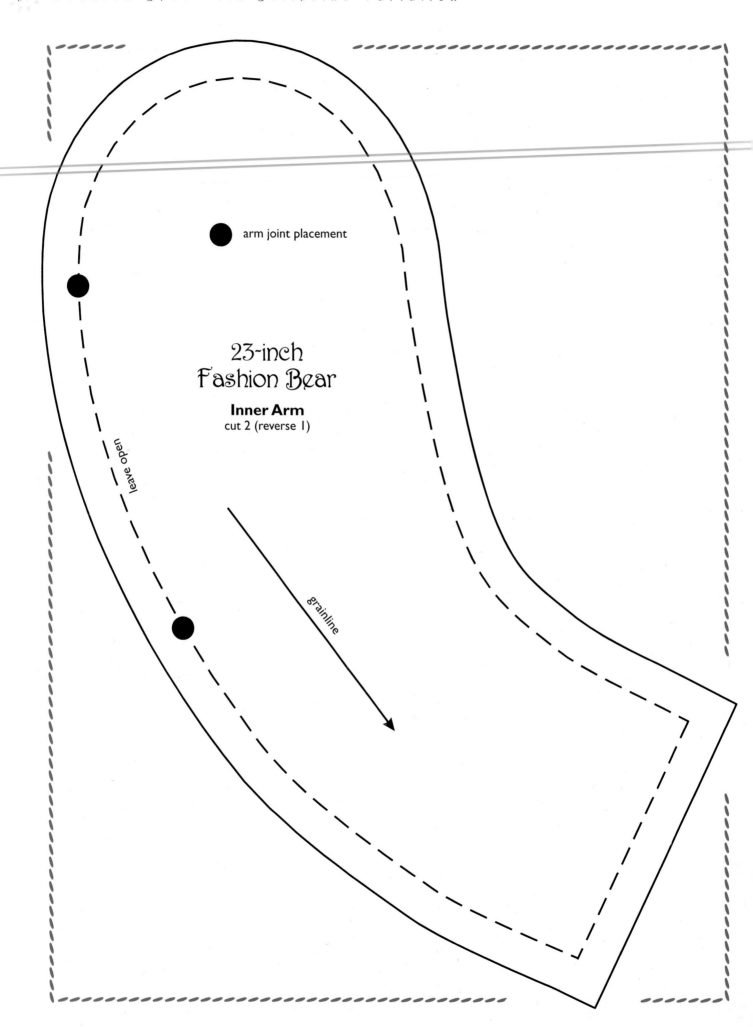

arm joint placement

23-inch
Fashion Bear

Inner Arm
cut 2 (reverse 1)

leave open

grainline

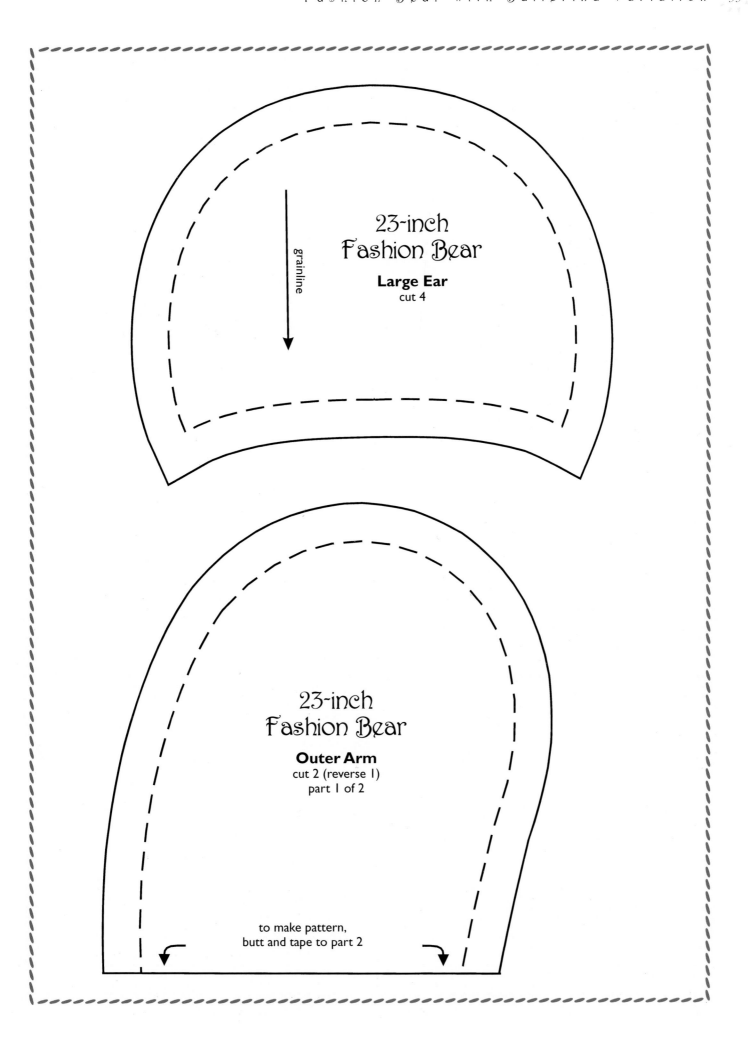

23-inch
Fashion Bear

Large Ear
cut 4

grainline

23-inch
Fashion Bear

Outer Arm
cut 2 (reverse 1)
part 1 of 2

to make pattern,
butt and tape to part 2

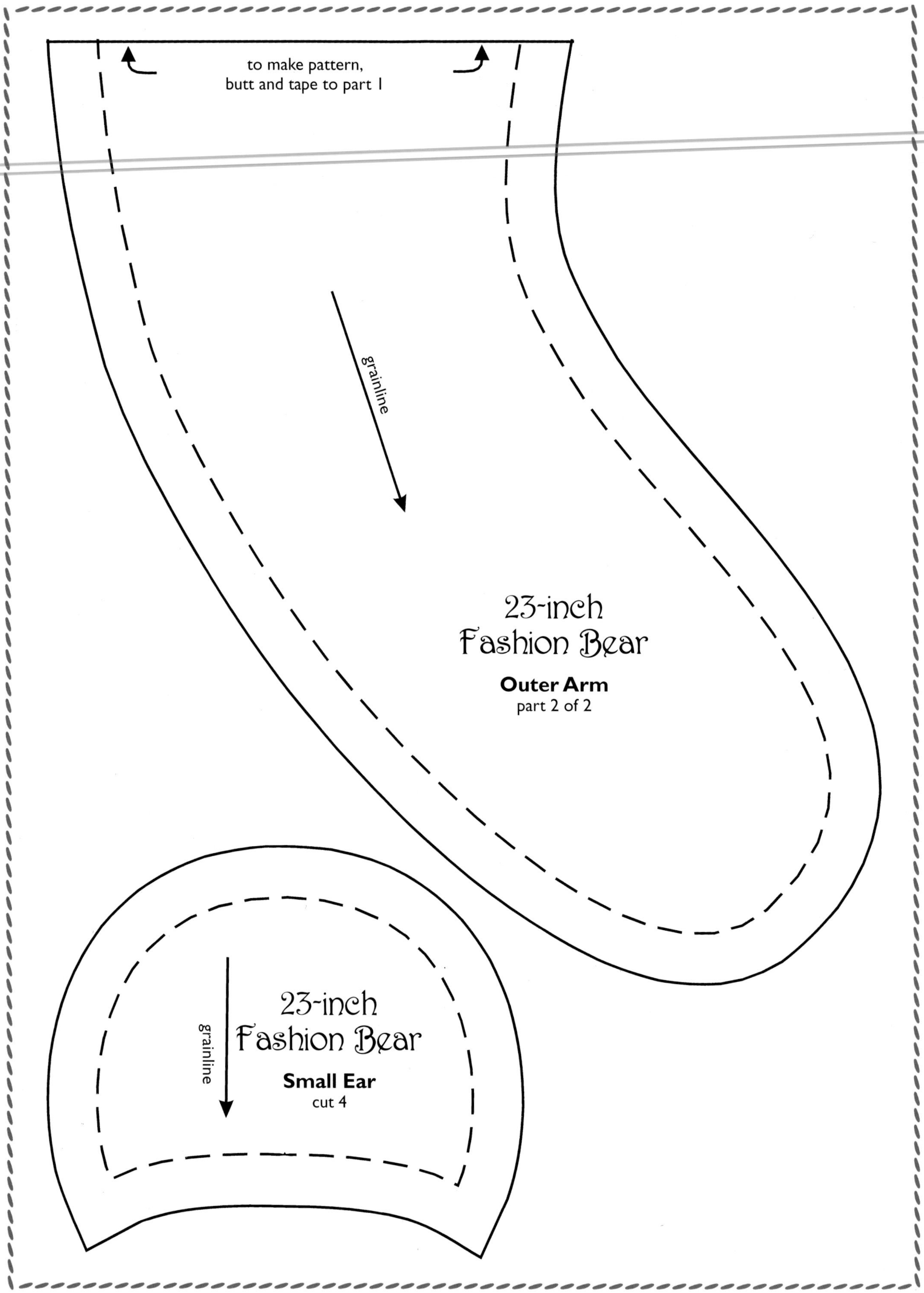

to make pattern,
butt and tape to part 1

grainline

23-inch
Fashion Bear

Outer Arm
part 2 of 2

23-inch
Fashion Bear

grainline

Small Ear
cut 4

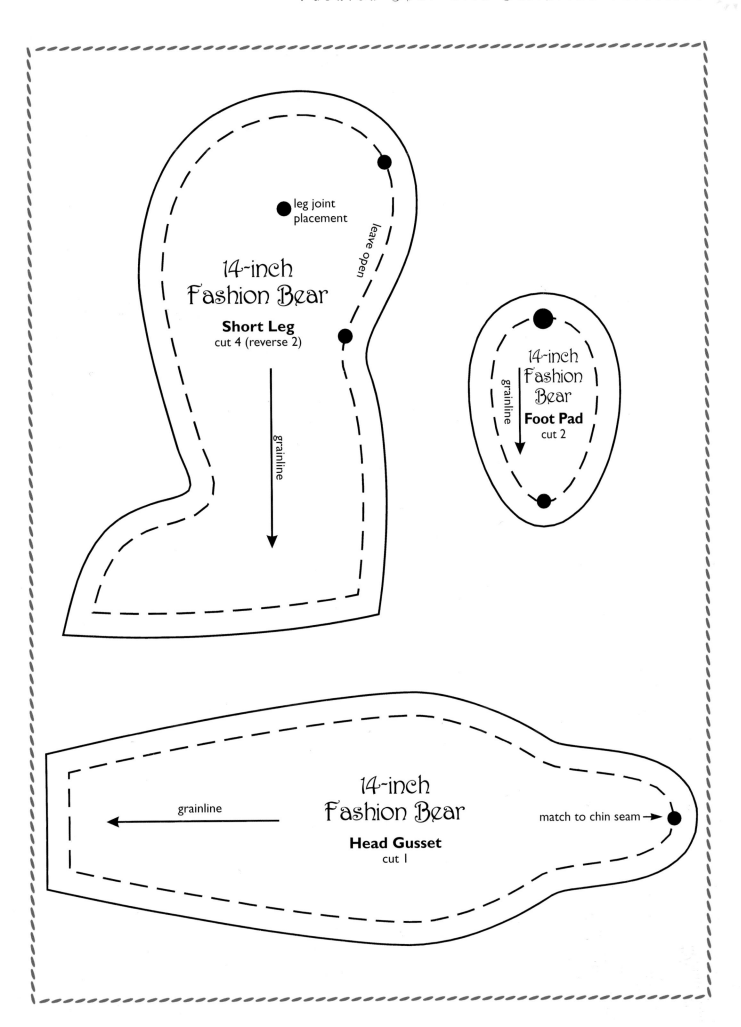

leg joint
placement

14-inch
Fashion Bear

Short Leg
cut 4 (reverse 2)

leave open

grainline

14-inch
Fashion
Bear

Foot Pad
cut 2

grainline

14-inch
Fashion Bear

Head Gusset
cut 1

grainline

match to chin seam

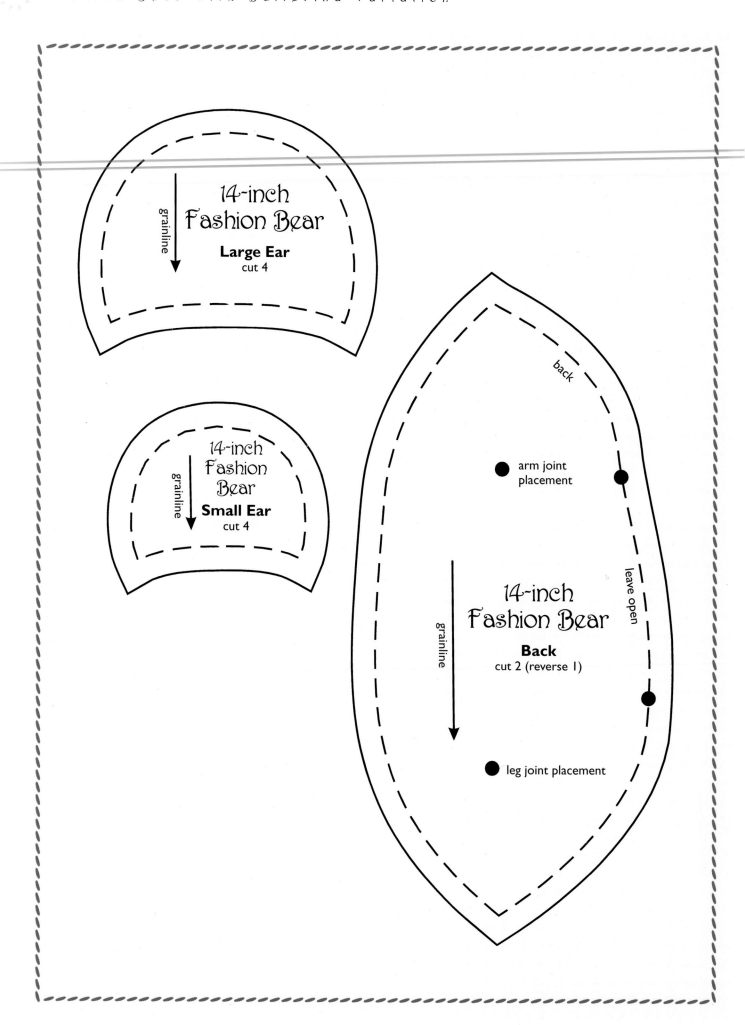

14-inch
Fashion Bear

Large Ear
cut 4

grainline

14-inch
Fashion
Bear

Small Ear
cut 4

grainline

back

● arm joint
placement

leave open

14-inch
Fashion Bear

Back
cut 2 (reverse 1)

grainline

● leg joint placement

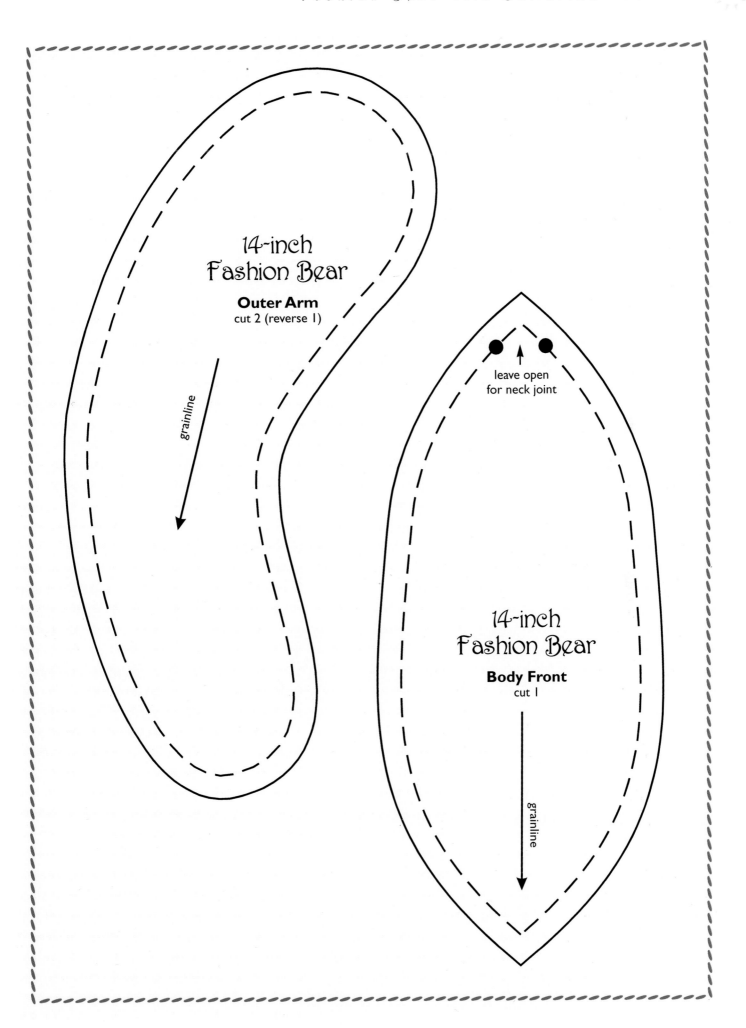

14-inch
Fashion Bear

Outer Arm
cut 2 (reverse 1)

grainline

leave open
for neck joint

14-inch
Fashion Bear

Body Front
cut 1

grainline

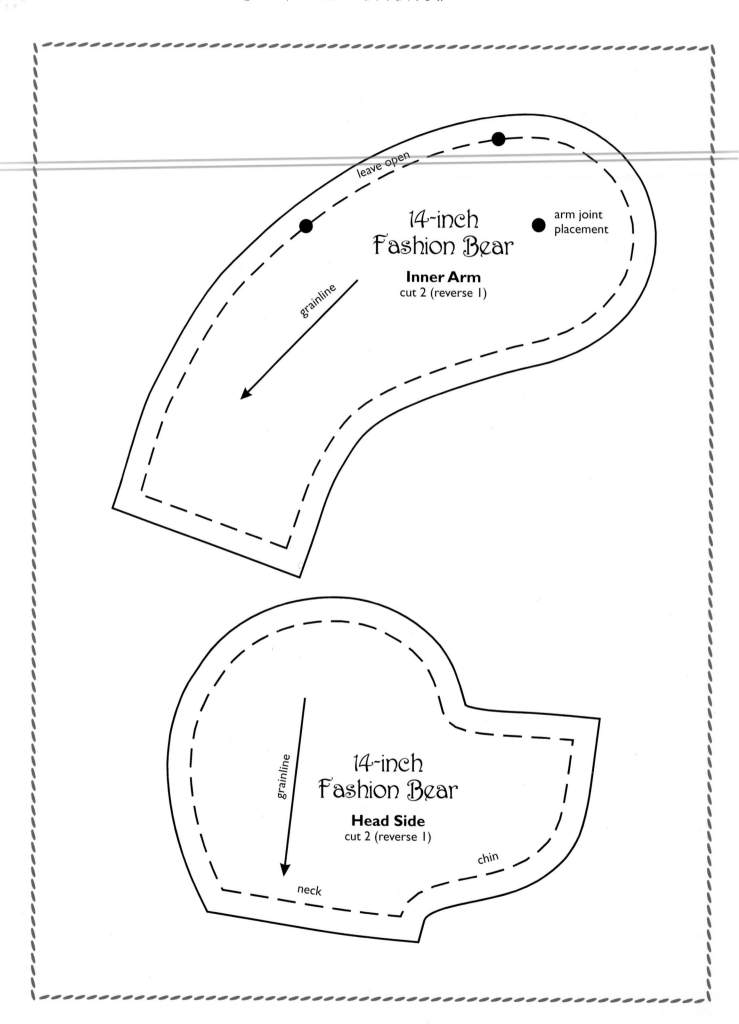

14-inch
Fashion Bear

Inner Arm
cut 2 (reverse 1)

leave open

arm joint
placement

grainline

14-inch
Fashion Bear

Head Side
cut 2 (reverse 1)

grainline

chin

neck

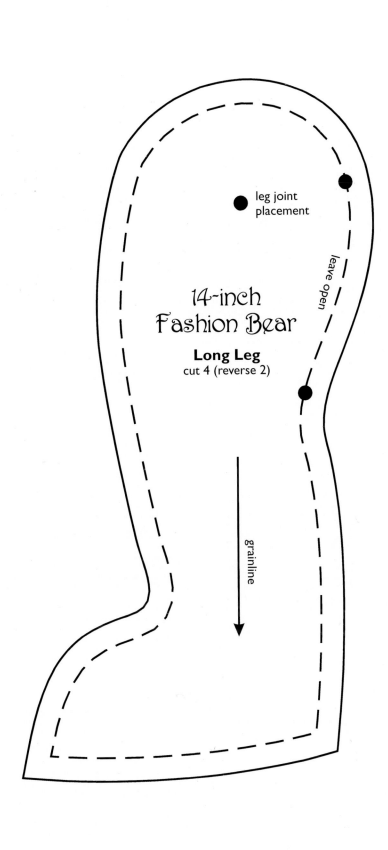

leg joint
placement

leave open

14-inch
Fashion Bear

Long Leg
cut 4 (reverse 2)

grainline

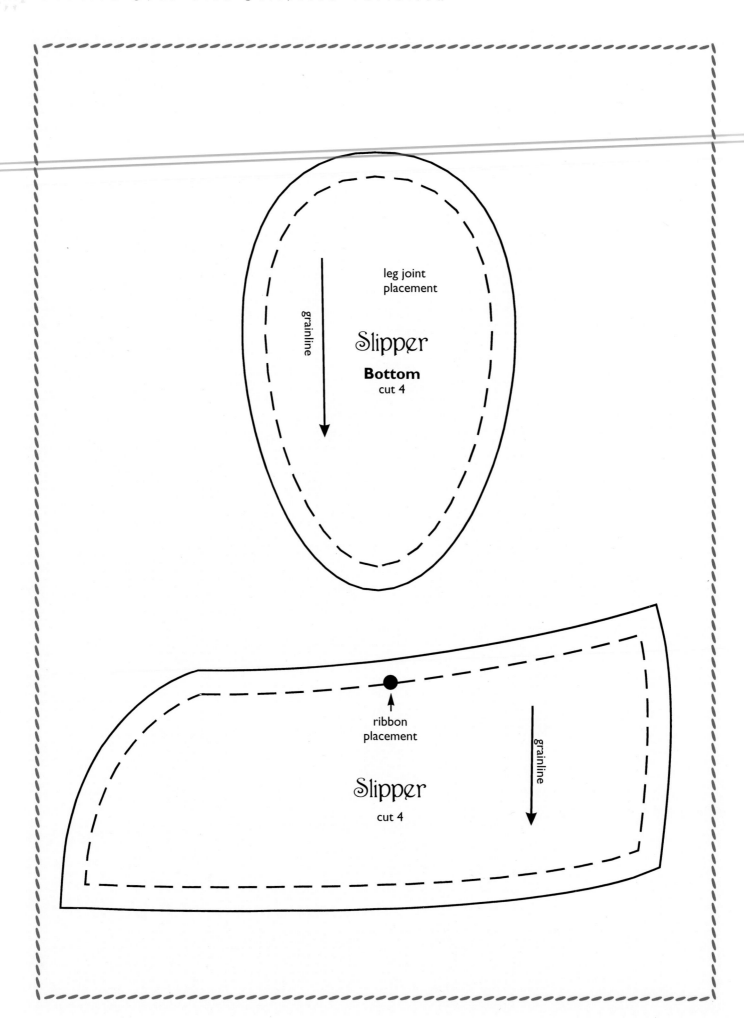

leg joint
placement

grainline

Slipper

Bottom
cut 4

ribbon
placement

grainline

Slipper

cut 4

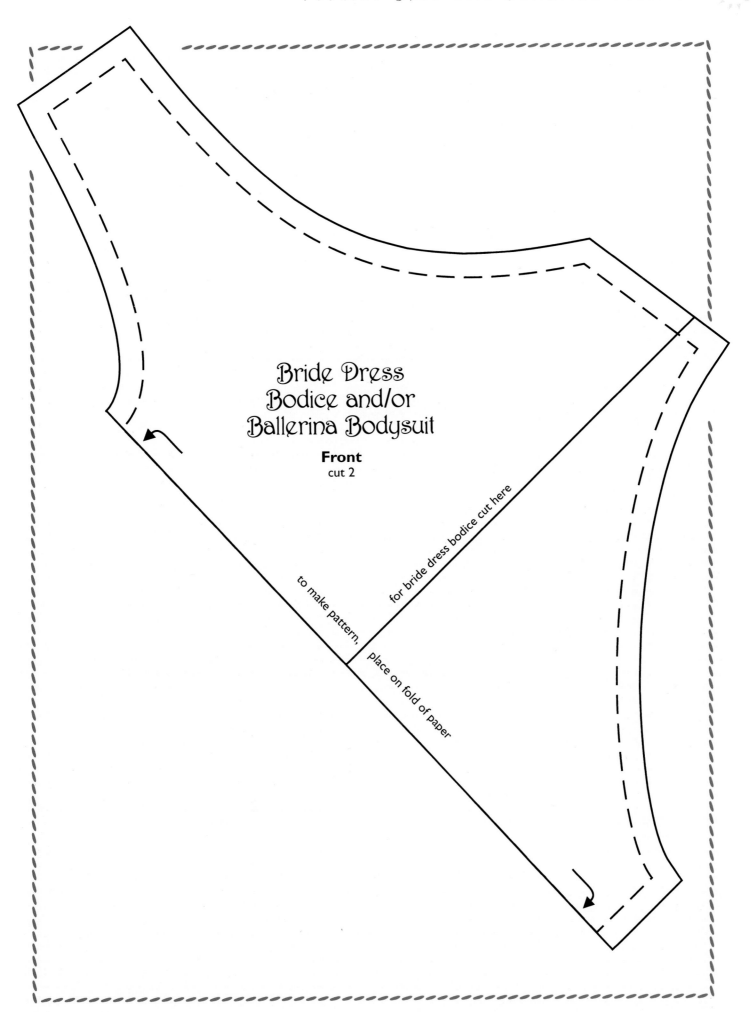

Bride Dress
Bodice and/or
Ballerina Bodysuit

Front
cut 2

for bride dress bodice cut here

to make pattern,

place on fold of paper

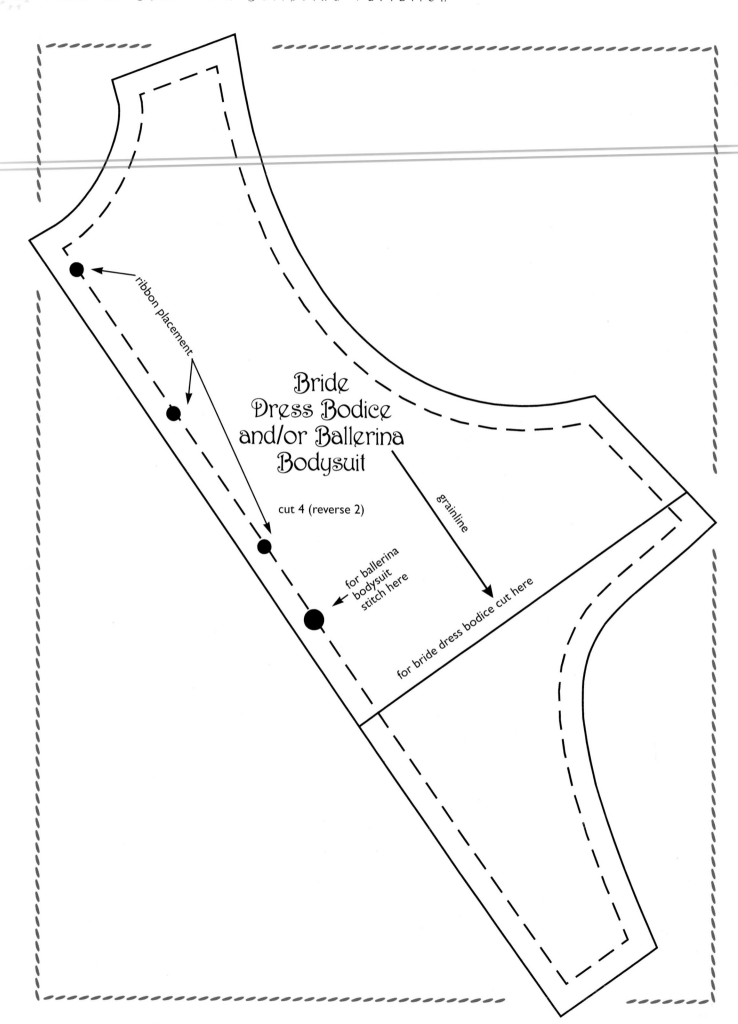

ribbon placement

Bride
Dress Bodice
and/or Ballerina
Bodysuit

cut 4 (reverse 2)

for ballerina
bodysuit
stitch here

grainline

for bride dress bodice cut here

Bride Dress Sleeve
cut 2

to make pattern, place on fold of paper

chapter seven

Small and Smaller Bears

Finished sizes:
Small Bear: 11 inches (27.9cm) • Smaller Bear: 9¼ inches (23.5cm)
Smallest Bear: 5½ inches (14cm)

As a final addition to your bear-making skills, this chapter contains

patterns for a bear in three sizes—from small to

mini. These Lilliputian bruins are just as easy to make as their larger

cousins, although the small size of the pattern pieces requires atten-

tive stitching. In addition, special considerations, such as

thread jointing and fabric choices for small bears, are addressed in this chapter.

materials

* **Fur fabric:**
  Small Bear: 12 × 21 inches
  (30.5 × 53.3cm)
  Smaller Bear: 8 × 18 inches
  (20.3 × 45.7cm)
  Smallest Bear: 8 × 10 inches
  (20.3 × 25.4cm)
* **Matching thread**
* **Piece of suede or wool felt
  for paw pads and soles
  (optional)**
* **Joints:**
  Small Bear: Five sets of
  1¼-inch (3.1cm) joints
  Smaller Bear: Five sets of
  ¾-inch (1.8cm) joints, or
  thread joint (see page 115)
  Smallest Bear: Thread joint
  (see page 115)
* **Eyes:**
  Small Bear: 10mm
  Smaller Bear: 7mm
  Smallest Bear: 3mm
* **Waxed dental floss or
  carpet thread**
* **Polyester fiberfill stuffing**
* **Perle cotton or embroidery
  floss**

**Bunny Bear (11 inches
[27.9cm])**
* **Fur fabric:**
  White: 12 × 21 inches
  (30.5 × 53.3cm)
  Brown: 8-inch (20.3cm)
  square
* **8-inch (20.3cm) square of
  pink lining fabric for hat**
* **¾ yard (68.5cm) of ½-inch
  (1.2cm) -wide ribbon**

instructions

*Note: All seam allowances are ⅛ inch
(3mm).*

1 Prepare the patterns, then mark
and cut out the fur as instructed on
pages 12 and 13.

2 Pin the two body pieces
together. Stitch, leaving an opening
between the dots at the back for
turning and stuffing. Turn the body
right side out.

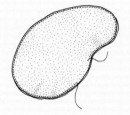

3 Right sides together, pin paw
pads, if used, to inner arms. Stitch.

4 Fold the arm along the foldline
so that the right sides are together.
Match the raw edges of the arm all
the way around. Pin. Stitch around
arm, leaving an opening between
the dots at the back of the arm for
turning and stuffing. Turn the arm
right side out. Repeat for the second arm.

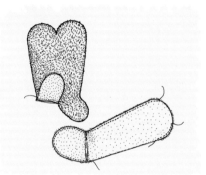

Special Considerations
for Small Bears

Due to their diminutive stature,
miniature bears require sewing and
fabric choices different from their
larger brothers and sisters.

To maintain a proper scale, short
pile fabrics are the best choice for
small bears. A ¼-inch (6mm) pile
looks fine on a smaller bear, and the
close nap of an upholstery fabric
(sold especially for teddies by the
suppliers listed in the Sources section on page 124) is just the right
scale for the miniest bears. Velvet
and velveteen work up beautifully as
well for these tiny bruins.

Likewise, a smaller seam allowance
is called for when working with small
bears. A ⅛-inch (3mm) seam allowance is compulsory.

Once the bear gets below 4
inches (10.2cm), machine stitching
becomes difficult, if not impossible.
Hand sewing is a better choice.
A simple overhand stitch, worked
closely, makes quick work of con-

structing these minis.

To facilitate turning
tiny body parts, try
inserting a hemostat into
the limb, grabbing a far bit of the
fabric and pulling the body part
right side out. Go slowly and use
great care.

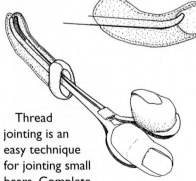

Thread
jointing is an
easy technique
for jointing small
bears. Complete
instructions are given on page 115.

Glass eyes are available in sizes
small enough for the bear patterns
here. Other options include beads
and buttons.

5 Fold one leg in half so that the right sides match. Stitch from the dot at the lower back of the thigh down the leg. Stitch from the remaining top dot to the bottom of the foot.

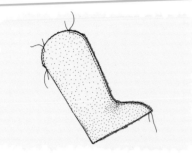

6 Pin the foot pads to the bottom of the feet, right sides together. Match the large dot on the foot pad to the front leg seam and the small dot to the back leg seam. Stitch, with the foot pad against the sewing machine bed. Turn the leg right side out.

7 Pin the two side head pieces together, right sides together, from the nose to the base of the neck. Stitch.

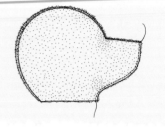

8 Pin the dot on the head gusset to the seam where the two head pieces meet at the tip of the nose. Pin one side of the gusset from the tip of the nose to the base of the neck, easing the gusset to fit as you go. Stitch. Repeat for the other side. Turn right side out.

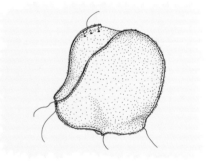

9 Match two ear pieces and stitch the rounded edges together, leaving the lower edges open. Turn. Turn raw edges under ¹/4 inch (6mm). Whipstitch closed. Repeat for the second ear.

10 If using safety eyes, install them now as instructed on page 46.

11 Stuff the head.

12 If using glass eyes, install them now as instructed on page 46.

13 Joint the head, arms, and legs. For the Small Bear, follow the instructions on page 44; for the

Smaller Bear and Smallest Bear, use thread joints (see below).

14 Stuff the body, arms, and legs. With a ladderstitch (see page 17), stitch the openings closed. If thread jointing, skip to the next step.

15 Decide where you want the ears. Pin them in place. Stitch the ears to the head in a circular motion, sewing through the ear at the top of the circle and the head on the bottom of the circle.

16 Embroider the nose and mouth as instructed on page 75.

17 If using beads for eyes, sew them in place now.

Thread Joints

Thread joints are a good choice where the small size of the bear makes hardware joints troublesome or impossible to install, and where the weight of many types of hardware joints would make a little bruin too hefty in proportion to his size.

Thread choices include carpet thread, heavy nylon thread, or waxed dental floss. A long dollmaker's needle is helpful; the length depends on the size of the bear.

Instructions

1. Stuff the head and close the neck opening. Stuff the arms, legs, and body. Close all openings. Finish the neck opening by gathering it closed.

2. Thread a dollmaker's needle and make a double knot in one end.

3. To joint the head, insert the needle into the base of the neck and out the top of the head. Go back into the head in the same hole the needle just emerged from and out the bottom. Push the needle into the top of the body at the marking and out the bottom. Go back into the same hole at the bottom of the body, through the neck, and out the top of the head. Pull the thread tight. Go back in the same hole at the top of the head and out the bottom of the body. Pull tight again. Make a knot in the thread an inch or two (2.5 or 5cm) where it emerges from the bear. Insert the needle into the hole it just emerged from and out anywhere on the bear's body. Pull tight, popping the knot into the body, thereby anchoring the knot in the body. Go back in the hole the needle just emerged from, come out anywhere. Trim the thread close to the fur.

4. Install the arms and legs in the same manner.

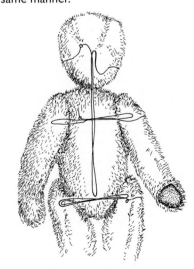

bunny bear

1 Follow the instructions for the Small Bear, making the head from the brown fur and the body, arms, and legs from the white fur. When preparing the patterns and cutting out the fur, cut out the bunny hat pieces.

2 Right sides together, seam two bunny ear pieces, leaving the straight edge open. Turn right side out.

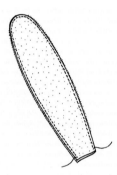

3 Right sides together, pin the bunny hat sides to the gusset. Fold the ears lengthwise and insert them into the seam at the dots as shown. Stitch, catching the ears in the seam. Pin and stitch the bunny hat lining side pieces to the lining gusset.

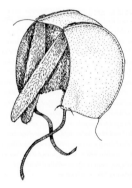

4 Cut the ribbon in half. Baste the ribbon pieces to the hat as shown.

5 Right sides together, pin the lining to the bunny hat along the front and back edges. Stitch, leaving a 1-inch (2.5cm) opening for turning. Turn right side out. Hand stitch the opening closed.

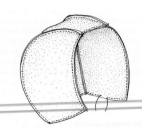

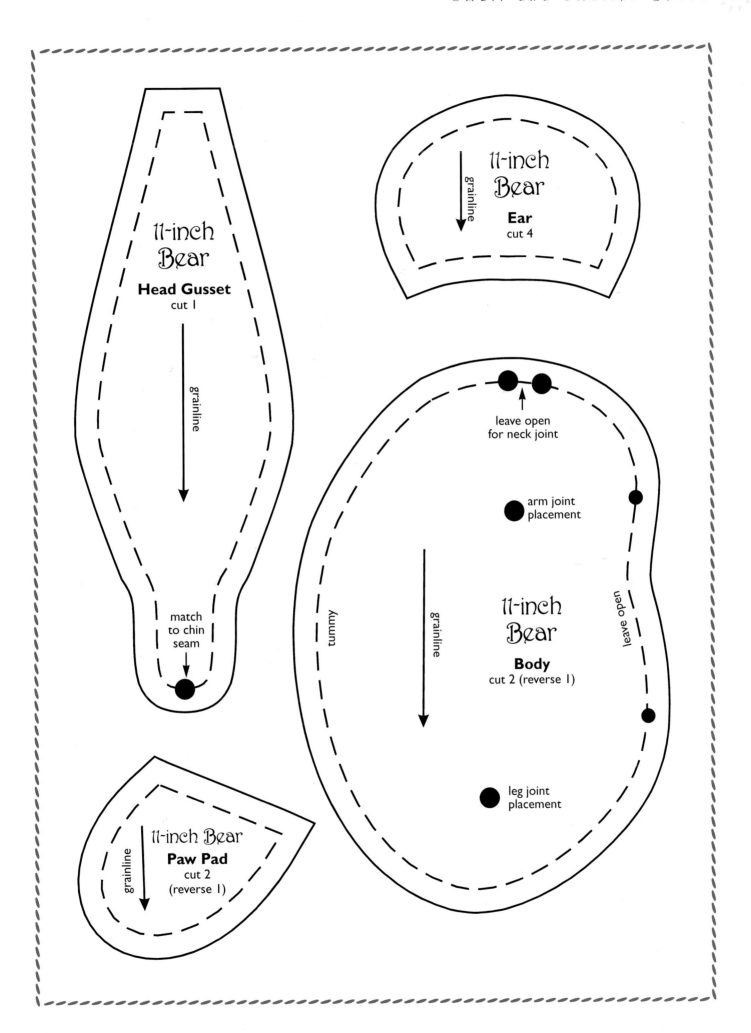

11-inch Bear
Head Gusset
cut 1

grainline

match to chin seam

11-inch Bear
Ear
cut 4

grainline

leave open for neck joint

arm joint placement

tummy

grainline

11-inch Bear
Body
cut 2 (reverse 1)

leave open

leg joint placement

11-inch Bear
Paw Pad
cut 2
(reverse 1)

grainline

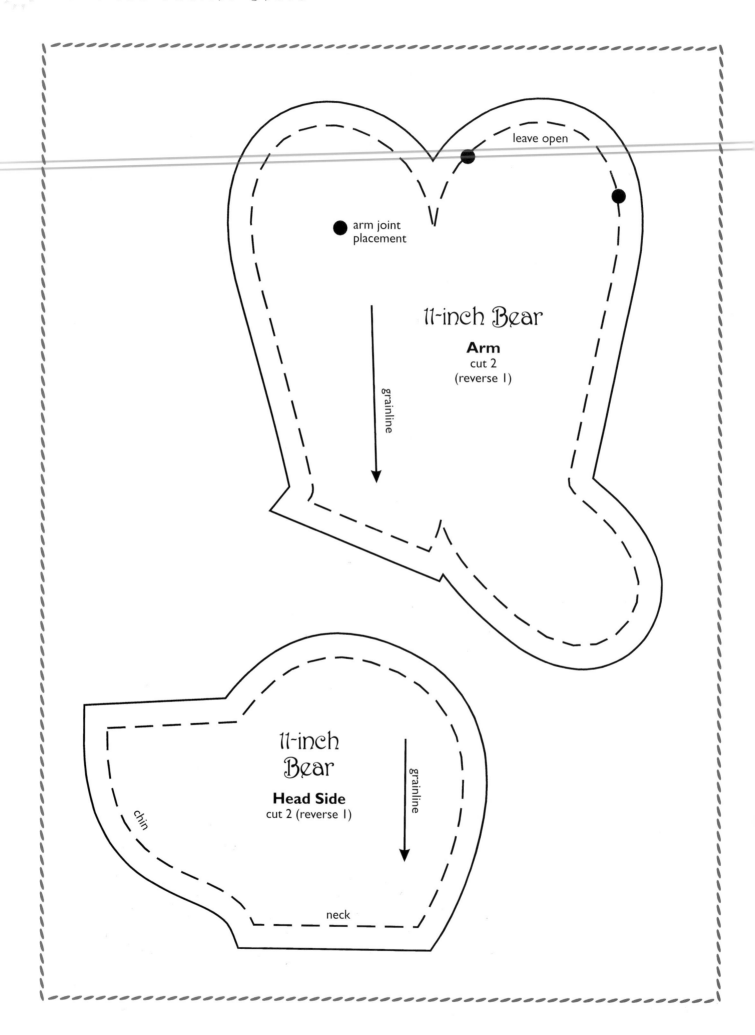

arm joint
placement

leave open

11-inch Bear

Arm
cut 2
(reverse 1)

grainline

11-inch
Bear

Head Side
cut 2 (reverse 1)

grainline

chin

neck

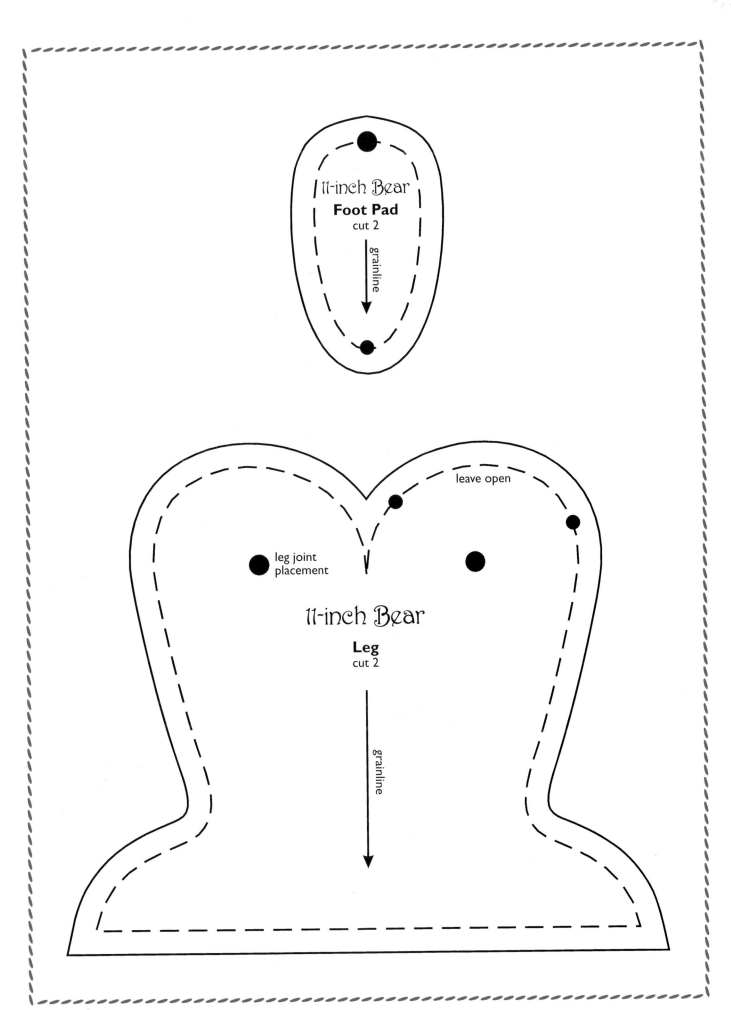

11-inch Bear
Foot Pad
cut 2

grainline

leave open

leg joint
placement

11-inch Bear

Leg
cut 2

grainline

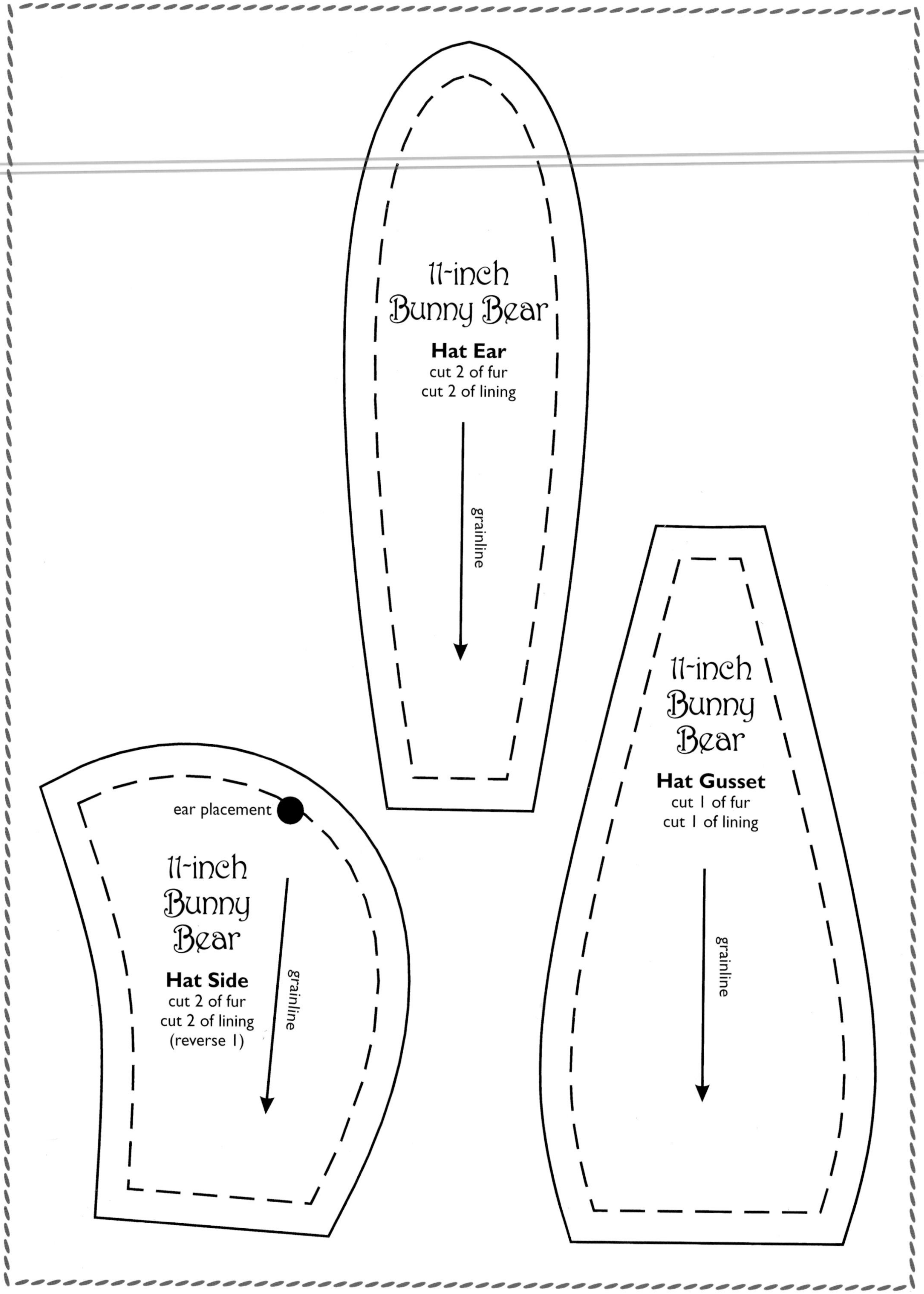

11-inch Bunny Bear

Hat Ear
cut 2 of fur
cut 2 of lining

grainline

11-inch Bunny Bear

Hat Gusset
cut 1 of fur
cut 1 of lining

grainline

ear placement

11-inch Bunny Bear

Hat Side
cut 2 of fur
cut 2 of lining
(reverse 1)

grainline

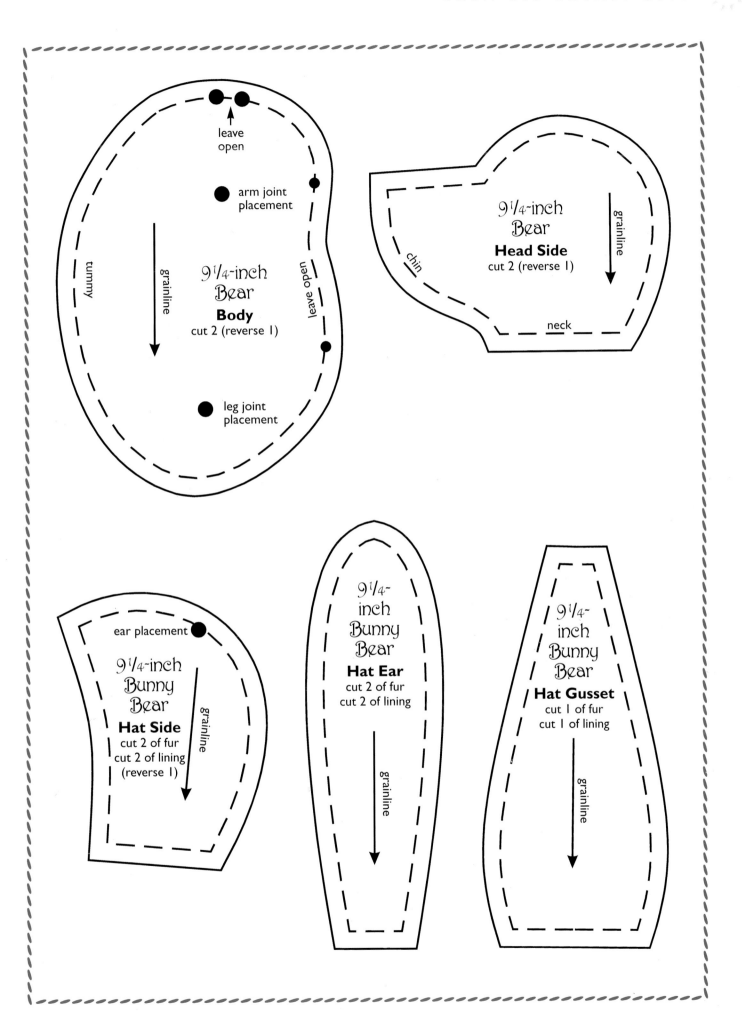

leave
open

arm joint
placement

tummy

grainline

9¼-inch
Bear
Body
cut 2 (reverse 1)

leave open

leg joint
placement

9¼-inch
Bear
Head Side
cut 2 (reverse 1)

grainline

chin

neck

ear placement

9¼-inch
Bunny
Bear
Hat Side
cut 2 of fur
cut 2 of lining
(reverse 1)

grainline

9¼-
inch
Bunny
Bear
Hat Ear
cut 2 of fur
cut 2 of lining

grainline

9¼-
inch
Bunny
Bear
Hat Gusset
cut 1 of fur
cut 1 of lining

grainline

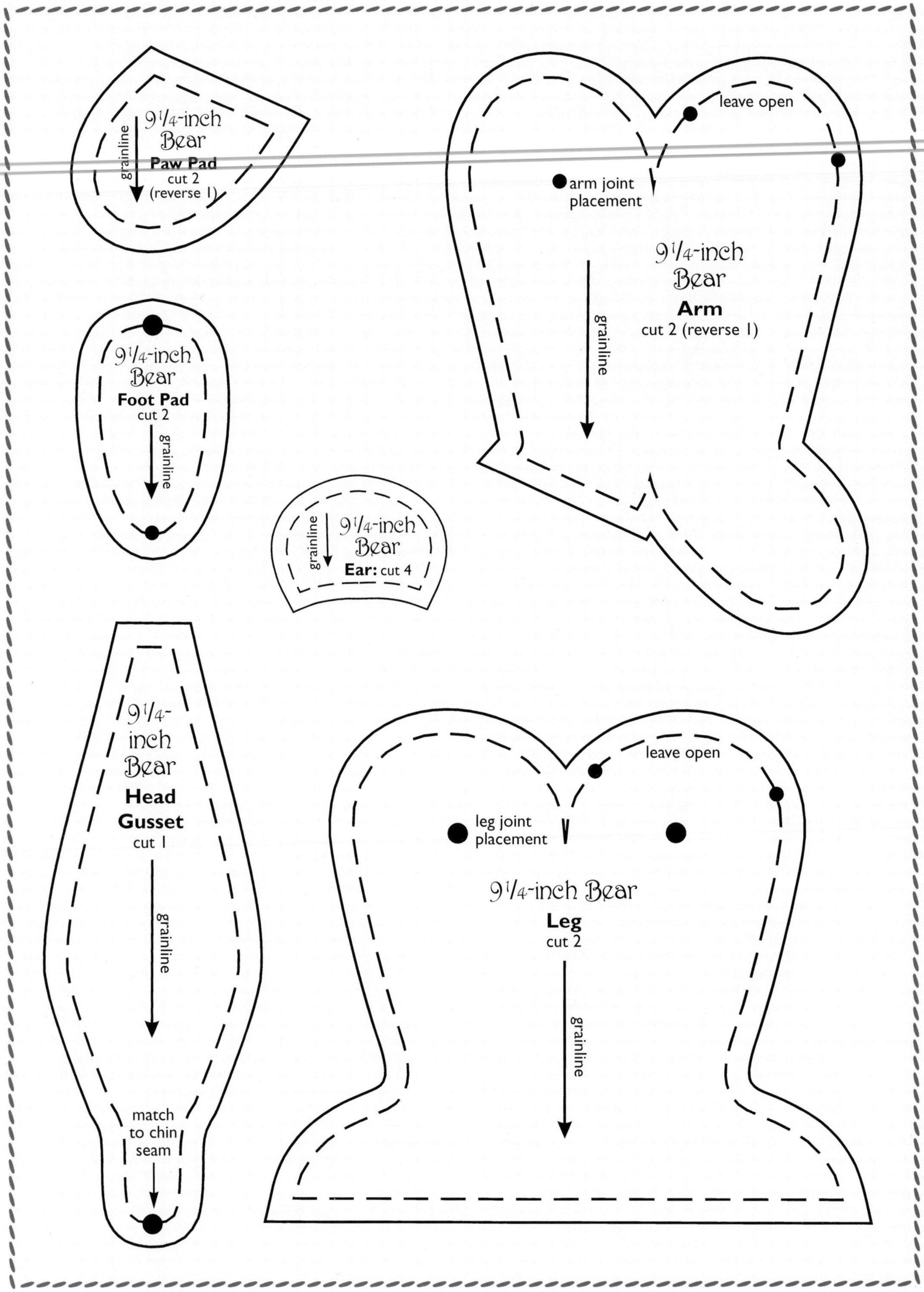

9¼-inch
Bear
Paw Pad
cut 2
(reverse 1)

grainline

leave open

● arm joint
placement

9¼-inch
Bear
Arm
cut 2 (reverse 1)

grainline

9¼-inch
Bear
Foot Pad
cut 2

grainline

grainline 9¼-inch
Bear
Ear: cut 4

9¼-
inch
Bear
**Head
Gusset**
cut 1

grainline

leave open

leg joint
placement

9¼-inch Bear
Leg
cut 2

grainline

match
to chin
seam

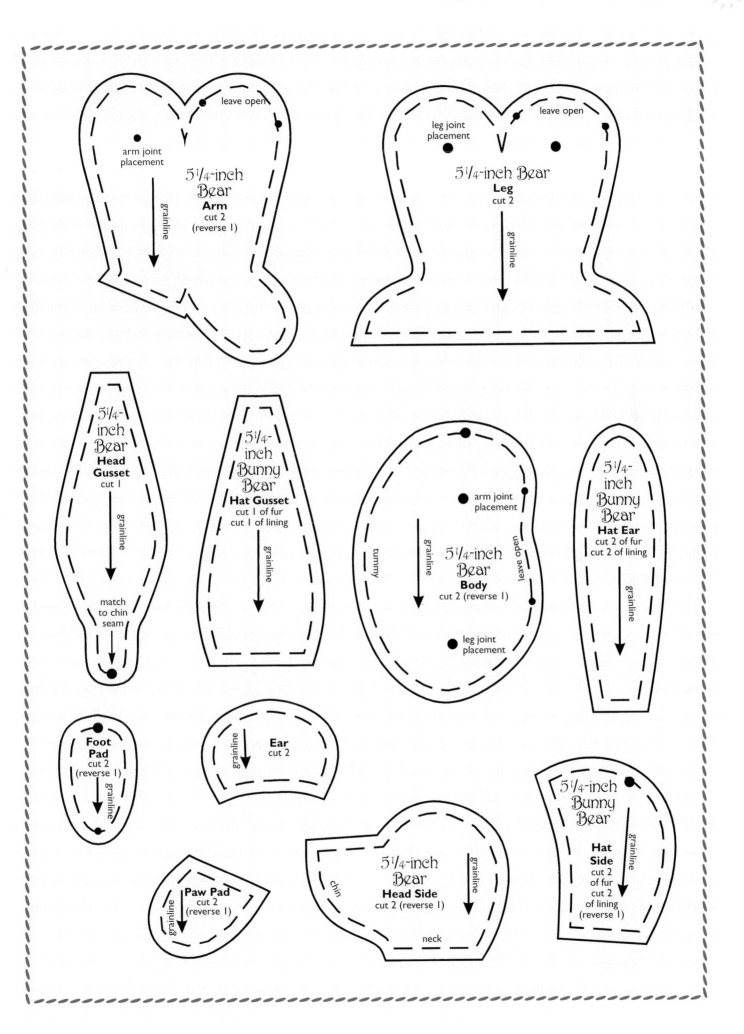

you are invited...

One of the most pleasurable elements of a teddy bear–making class—besides the utter magic of the bears themselves—is the comaraderie of the students. Swapping ideas, sharing the learning process, and making new friendships compound the joy of creating a bear.

I invite you to share the joy of bear making through mail. You can send photographs of your bears and letters describing your bears and bear making to me at the address below. Whether you use my patterns as is, modify them, or choose different materials, or make up your own designs, I will enjoy meeting you and your bears.

Jodie Davis

Jodie Davis Publishing, Inc.
15 West 26th Street
New York, NY 10010

email: CompuServe: 73522,2430;
GEnie: J.DAVIS60

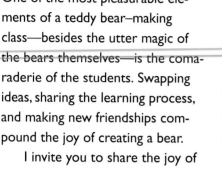

sources

Bear Clawset
27 Palermo Walk
Long Beach, CA 90803
(310) 434-8077
Catalog: $3.50 or $4.50 outside U.S.

Bear-making supplies.

by Diane
1126 Ivon Avenue
Endicott, NY 13760-1431
(607) 754-0391
Catalog: $2.00 or $3.50 outside U.S.

Bear supplies and patterns as well as patterns for a large selection of stuffed animals.

Edinburgh Imports, Inc.
P.O. Box 722
Woodland Hills, CA 91365-0722
1-800-EDINBRG
Catalog: Two first-class stamps

Wonderful selection of everything you need for bear making. Inquire about the samples of delicious imported furs.

Intercal
1760 Monrovia, suite 17-A
Costa Mesa, CA 92627
(714) 645-9396
Catalog: Two first-class stamps

Bear-making supplies and imported furs.

bibliography

Davis, Jodie. *Easy-to-Make Teddy Bears and All the Trimmings.* Charlotte, Vt.: Williamson Publishing, Inc., 1988.

Maddigan, Judi. *Learn Bearmaking.* Menlo Park, Calif.: Open Chain Publishing, 1989.

Menten, Ted. *The Teddy Bear Lovers Catalog.* Philadelphia: Running Press, 1985.

———. *Teddy's Bearzaar.* Philadelphia: Running Press, 1988.

Index